BIBLE

ROMANS

 **Week Books**

10WeekBooks.com

ROMANS: A 10 WEEK BIBLE STUDY

Scriptures taken from the Holy Bible, New International Version®, NIV®. Copyright © 1973, 1978, 1984, 2011 by Biblica, Inc.™ Used by permission of Zondervan. All rights reserved worldwide. www.zondervan.com   The "NIV" and "New International Version" are trademarks registered in the United States Patent and Trademark Office by Biblica, Inc.™

ISBN: 0-9997312-2
ISBN-13: 978-0-9997312-2-2

Cover: Apse mosaic of the Basilica of Saint Paul Outside the Walls (1220) - Rome - Italy

10WeekBooks.com

For Tessa

Born on 4/18/2018 at 4:18pm, you are truly a sign and a wonder from the Lord to your mother and I. We pray that your life will reflect the incomparable good news of the gospel of Jesus as He put it:

"The Spirit of the Lord is on me,
because he has anointed me
to proclaim good news to the poor.
He has sent me to proclaim freedom for the prisoners
and recovery of sight for the blind,
to set the oppressed free,
to proclaim the year of the Lord's favor."

Luke 4:18-19

CONTENTS

ABOUT THE 10 WEEK BIBLE STUDY

My heart is to see people fall in love with God through growing in His Word. The 10 Week Bible Study helps people do that through repetition, helpful commentary and engaging questions. Most of all, this study helps people stay engaged by encouraging them to keep going when they get off track, get confused or get lost.

David, in Psalm 1, told us that if we meditated on God's Word day and night, we would be like a tree planted by rivers of living water. I don't know about you, but I find it hard to remember to meditate at all hours of the day. The 10 Week Bible Study makes that easy by encouraging people to read the book of the Bible being studied 10 times in 10 weeks (hence the name).

When you start reading God's Word like that, you'll find that you accidentally meditate on His Word. In those moments when your mind is at rest and blank, it always snaps to something you've been thinking about. When you pull up to the stoplight, maybe your mind goes to work, chores or that show you've been binging on Netflix lately. With the 10 Week Bible Study, you'll find yourself thinking about God's Word in those moments. You may just catch yourself asking God questions about what you've been reading without even thinking about it.

That is what David meant by meditating on God's Word day and night, that your heart and mind are so full of His Word that you can't help but think about it in those quiet times.

ADDITIONAL RESOURCES

Join the growing community of people who listen, watch and discuss the 10 Week Bible Study online. With millions of downloads and thousands of free resources to choose from, the 10 Week Bible Study produces daily podcasts, videos and other downloadable content to help you grow in your walk with God.

For more information and to join our email list to get regular encouragement in God's Word, visit 10WeekBible.com today.

Introduction to Romans

As an author I feel wholly inadequate to comment on Romans because of the weight that so many before me have esteemed this book with. I do not take writing on any book of the Bible lightly, but I feel an especially strong weight of obligation to treat Romans with great care and dignity. It has been the book that has swayed many a "sinner" and self-righteous Pharisee alike.

The concepts in Romans are deep, but understandable. The book includes ideas held in the tension of life, but it is within those tensions that our Christian walk exists. Things like the tension between the flesh and the spirit, works and grace and our will and God's sovereignty are what we find in Romans.

It is because of this that a new crop of teachings have arisen in the past decade or two that try to alleviate people from that tension, each growing more perverse with time, distorting this beautiful grace as expressed in Romans. It is because of these teachings I feel compelled to add one more book to the catalogue of heaven to cover it.

OUTLINE OF ROMANS

Chapters 1-2
    Everyone's a sinner

Chapters 3-8
    Law v. Grace | Sin v. Justification

Chapters 9-11
    Israel v. The Gentiles

Chapters 12-15
    Loving Well

Chapters 16
    Final Greetings

ROMANS IN 10 WEEKS

ROMANS 1

STUDY QUESTIONS

1. What is it that Paul hopes to teach the Gentiles?

2. Why do you think Paul wanted to visit Rome so badly?

3. What are we saved by today? What were people in the Old Testament saved by?

4. What is God's wrath? Why do you think Paul starts a book about salvation by grace through faith with the concept of wrath?

5. Why do you think God gives people over to their sinful desires instead of just destroying them?

6. What is the root cause of all the different kinds of sinfulness that Paul lists in chapter one?

7. Do you ever find yourself trying to self-justify your sin? If so, what steps can you take to instead agree with God's requirements and seek His grace?

COMMENTARY NOTES

ROMANS CHAPTER 1

Romans is an all-important book of scripture for the New-Testament believer. Thousands of wayward sinners and self-righteous religious people alike have found refuge and redemption within its pages for nearly two thousand years. It brings to the forefront our great need for the grace and salvation of Jesus Christ, the message of the eternal gospel.

AUTHOR AND DATE

The Apostle Paul is the author of Romans. His name is the first word of the book, to take credit for its contents as he dictated it to his friend Tertius (16:22). Many scholars believe that Romans was written while he was in the city of Corinth sometime in the mid 50's AD.

APOSTLESHIP
1:1-7

Paul begins Romans by saying that the apostleship given to him was for the purpose of calling all Gentiles to obedience through faith. He did not say salvation through faith, but obedience. We often say that it was the point of Jesus' sacrifice to save us, but it was in fact to give us the power to obey God, something we were helpless to do before salvation. It is our obedience to this "new" law of justification through faith that Paul will expound on that is our source of salvation.

Obedience, in the Old Testament and New Testament, is and has always been the standard by which we are judged before God. To the contrary of freeing us from obedience, as many today claim Romans teaches, Paul will tell us that obedience is foundational to our salvation. It is the nature and definition of that obedience that Paul will define throughout the book of Romans. *What* we must be obedient to is where Romans defines itself.

Throughout Romans, Paul lays out the case that we will always be subject to one law or another. One will bring death and one will bring life, so why not choose to obey the law that brings life?

VISITING ROME
1:8-17

It is amazing to think that the Roman church's faith was being reported all over the world. Perhaps it was because no one would have expected to find faith in such a dark place as Rome. Whatever the reason, Paul really wants to visit these saints to find out what's going on. Paul will speak in Romans 15 about only desiring to go and work where no one has worked before, but something about the Roman church continues to draw him. He longs to visit them, and eventually he would, just not under the best of circumstances—he will live under house arrest in Rome for two years (Acts 28:30).

Paul knows that when he comes to Rome he has things he can impart to them. Far from arrogance, Paul understands who he is and his calling before the Lord. He also acknowledges that he can learn and be encouraged by them as well. We all have something unique that we "bring to the table" in the church. The Lord has given us all the same grace, but He has never created two people exactly alike. We need each other and Paul is acknowledging that here.

Paul talks about how he is "obligated" to both Greeks and non-Greeks. First, this is not a reference to Jews and Gentiles, but to those within the Roman world (Greeks) and those outside (non-Greeks). This obligation he speaks of is the commission he was given by God to be an apostle to the Gentiles. "Greeks and non-Greeks" is a phrase he is using to encompass all Gentiles outside Israel as a Greco-Roman audience would have understood them.

SALVATION BY FAITH
1:16-17

Paul is going to immediately juxtapose this by saying that this salvation he is so eager to preach is effective for salvation to Jews first. There is no doubt here what Paul is saying: that salvation has come first to the Jews. It is a gift of grace to the Gentiles that they are allowed into this relationship that God ordained from the time of Abraham to come through His chosen children, the

Israelites.

This is no small point in Romans. Whereas we will see that strict adherence to the law is not what will save now (nor was it what would save before Jesus), it is still to the children of Israel that salvation was intended. We, as Gentiles (if you are in fact a Gentile), will be "grafted in," as Paul will explain later in Romans.

Paul quotes from the Old Testament here to introduce this notion of salvation by grace through faith, the overriding theme of Romans.

> *See, the enemy is puffed up;*
>
> *his desires are not upright—*
>
> *but the righteous person will live by his faithfulness*
>
> *Habakkuk 2:4*

This salvation through faith is not a new idea that came from the sacrifice of Jesus, but the reality that those living under the law were to supposed to understand as well. Paul will continue to further develop this narrative throughout Romans.

GOD'S WRATH
1:18-20

Paul transitions very quickly from this introduction of the work of salvation by grace through faith into a very different topic: wrath. The last part of chapter one and much of chapter two will deal with God's wrath, something that seems contrary to the salvation Paul wants to spend much of Romans on.

Wrath, however, is a necessary component of understanding the salvation that Jesus has provided us. We have no salvation if it weren't for God's wrath. If there was no wrath and punishment from God, then there would be nothing to save us from. Salvation only comes if we are being saved from something. That something is a very contentious topic

Throughout history, as well as today, people have struggled with the notion of God's wrath. Our sinful natures want to do everything to self-justify: we want to prove to ourselves that we're not all that bad. But God's truth reveals otherwise.

Paul says that God's wrath is revealed against godlessness and wickedness. He says this as if we can look around and see it happening, which is exactly what he means. The rest of this chapter will be Paul explaining how God's wrath is not so hard to see if you are willing to look. The problem is that people don't want to look. They don't want to see it. We want to think that what we do is okay, like in the Old Testament when it said:

> In those days Israel had no king; everyone did as they saw fit.

> *Judges 21:25*

We, as human beings, have a serious problem with our own self-justification. Paul says that what we can know about God has been made plain to us by creation itself. It is so clear that he says we are all without excuse. We cannot reasonably deny that there is a God and we all know by nature that He must have requirements. By not seeking them out to follow, we show our utter contempt and rebellion against Him. Paul is taking away any argument that "we didn't know."

WRATH REVEALED
1:21-32

Paul tells us that people refuse to glorify God and give Him thanks. This is the primary way people show their contempt for God: by refusing to thank Him. We have an incurable entitlement mentality. Our sin nature causes us to feel like we are owed this life we live. God, however, demands that we honor and acknowledge Him as the author and creator of this life we have. It is this refusal to acknowledge our life-giver that reveals our true rebellion.

It is that rebellion that draws attention to the reality of God's wrath. It is hard to accept this notion of God's wrath if you are fundamentally comfortable in your own rebellion and self-justification. It is for this reason that God will give people over to their own destruction, as Paul goes on to explain.

Paul starts by explaining that people claimed to be wise by making their own gods, fashioned out of earthly materials and resembling created objects. It is in this act that people express their foolishness and rebellion. What comes next is actually quite shocking.

Instead of destroying the people who chose to do this, God was instead patient with them. It would have been completely within the rights of the creator of the universe to end the lives that would choose to worship something other than Him and convince others to do the same. But God doesn't destroy them; He actually lets them have and do what they want.

Paul tells us that God gave those wanting to live in sin over to their chosen lifestyle. He says that one of the first ways that sinfulness is expressed is through sexual immorality. Anything outside of a bonded marriage relationship between a man and a woman is considered sin in scripture, and it is dishonest to suggest otherwise.

He who commits adultery lacks sense; he who does it destroys himself.

Proverbs 6:32 ESV

"You shall not commit adultery.

Exodus 20:14 ESV

Therefore a man shall leave his father and his mother and hold fast to his wife, and they shall become one flesh.

Genesis 2:24 ESV

Let marriage be held in honor among all, and let the marriage bed be undefiled, for God will judge the sexually immoral and adulterous.

Hebrews 13:4 ESV

You shall not lie with a male as with a woman; it is an abomination.

Leviticus 18:22 ESV

If a man lies with a male as with a woman, both of them have committed an abomination; they shall surely be put to death; their blood is upon them.

Leviticus 20:13 ESV

Just as Sodom and Gomorrah and the surrounding cities, which likewise indulged in sexual immorality and pursued unnatural desire, serve as an example by undergoing a punishment of eternal fire.

Jude 1:7 ESV

The fact that there is such energy to prove that the Bible has never been against such lifestyles is proof itself of what Paul is saying here. Those who try to justify another lifestyle of sin, especially those who use the Bible to do it, show the world that they have already been given over to their sinful desires by God.

The reason why sexual scandals are so common in our society is because God is being kind in exposing the first type of sin people rush toward. He is offering them a way out before they progress further down the path of rebellion. Continued sexual sin and a denial of God's righteous decrees go hand in hand. It is impossible to live in unrepentant sexual sin for any length of time before it becomes necessary to redefine what sin is.

If people refuse to repent at this stage, Paul tells us that the sinfulness continues in increasingly unhealthy ways. Next come what Paul calls "shameful" lusts. It is clear that he is speaking of homosexuality in verses 26 and 27. He then says that those people who engaged in such things received within themselves the due penalty for such sin and rebellion.

Sexual deviancy almost always results in literal, physical consequences. Although proverbial in nature—not every single person may have problems—we see clearly that as this deviancy increases, society suffers. We have seen an explosion of diseases that are transmitted primarily through sexual encounters, especially in those that are prone to cause injury to the body. This is exactly what Paul is speaking of. There are numerous accounts in Roman history of mental disorders being attributed to venereal diseases (sexually transmitted diseases).

Paul continues on that if there is no repentance, it grows even worse. From sexual perversion to societal acceptance and involvement in homosexuality, God will give those who continue in rebellion over to even worse things their hearts desire.

Next comes a "depraved mind." Paul gets less specific here, but we see that what he calls "wickedness, evil, greed and depravity" expresses itself in things like envy, murder, strife, deceit and malice. He says that as people grow more rebellious, not only do they partake in greater wickedness, they actually approve of others who join them. Paul says that such people deserve death—this wrath of God that he has been speaking of.

All the specific sins, however, are not the reason that people deserve the wrath of God. The sins are symptoms of the true problem. The reason is what Paul started out explaining; that we are rebellious by nature. We would rather worship things made by our own hands than worship the God who created us and those things. We want to justify ourselves so that we can convince ourselves we don't need God nor do we owe Him anything.

We owe God all honor, all respect, all glory and everything we have, if for no other reason, for creating us. Anything less is, by definition, rebellion against God our Creator.

For the self-righteous who feel they don't deserve God's wrath because they don't struggle with any of these things, Paul has much more to say in chapter two.

Don't forget to read Romans this week!
Visit 10WeekBible.com for more resources including daily podcasts, videos and more.

2

ROMANS 2-3

STUDY QUESTIONS

1. What is self-justification, and how does God feel about it? Do you feel like you ever self-justify your actions?

2. What is the Law that Paul keeps referring to? Why is it important?

3. How does a religious person store up the wrath of God for themselves?

4. Why did circumcision matter to the Israelites in the Old Testament? Why should it matter to us today?

5. What is the advantage of being a Jew if we are all saved by grace?

6. What is wrong with planning to sin and repent later? Do you remember a time when you may have done that?

7. How are Jews saved? How are Gentiles saved? Have you ever done that? If so, when? If not, will you consider it now?

COMMENTARY NOTES

ROMANS CHAPTER 2

JUDGING
2:1-4

Paul has spent the past several passages speaking of the judgment of the Lord against those who reject God and give themselves to sin. It may seem odd, then, that he now turns his attention to those who would presume to judge others, but there is more going on than meets the eye.

Paul seems to be speaking to people, Jews in particular, who ironically pass judgment on those who fit the descriptions in chapter one. They are people who refuse to repent and turn their hearts back to God, but for different reasons than those in chapter one.

We learned that because people refused to acknowledge God and rebelled against Him, He gave them over to their wickedness. In chapter two we see that there is another form of godlessness, and it comes from people who claim to know God and live by a set of agreed-upon rules that have nothing to do with God's righteous decrees. Paul says that these people are casting judgment on the chapter one crowd while thinking they are righteous, but are, in fact, just as bad off as those they judge.

This brings us back to the reality of mankind's bent toward self-justification. One way or another, people tend toward finding a way to justify how they want to live. With the pagan crowd, they convince themselves that there is no God, or that at the very least, that He is either no good or not really in charge. With the religious crowd, they create rules that may or may not be based on God's commands that fit nicely into the lifestyle they already lead.

The leaders of Israel at the time, the Pharisees, created rules that worked incredibly well for them. It allowed them, under the right circumstances, to divorce and remarry, commit adultery and fornication, steal from others and treat their parents with contempt, all while simultaneously allowing them to cast judgment on others who did the same sorts of things. Paul seems to have this kind of lifestyle in mind as he begins chapter two.

STORING UP WRATH
2:5-11

Paul continues to chastise this religious crowd by warning them that their identical unrepentant heart is causing them to store up wrath for themselves—no different than the people described in chapter one did. Paul also tells us that there is a day coming, called the "day of God's wrath." This is speaking of two potential times. The first is the actual end times, where God pours out His great wrath on the earth that has rejected Him and killed His people; those called by His name. The other inference is for those who don't live long enough to see the end times, they will one day meet God face to face, and if they have rejected Him or His ways, their meeting will be one of wrath.

Paul then goes on to compare and contrast those who "do good" (7) through persistence will be granted eternal life, but those who "follow evil" will inherit wrath and anger. The key phrase in understanding what Paul is saying here is not that it is solely our actions that determine our eternal outcome. It is this phrase about those "who reject the truth" (8).

This judgment is not determined primarily by our actions, how many good or bad things we have done, but by our choice of accepting or rejecting the truth—the truth that God is our creator and His Son Jesus is the only way to gain acceptance with Him. That choice, however, does impact our actions. Scripture is replete with stories and examples of how making the right choice to follow God has a dramatic impact on how we behave, while making a choice to reject Him leads to death and destruction through sinful lifestyles.

Paul is stating that these actions are a result of our choice of accepting or rejecting Jesus, not the means of getting there. Grace will lead us down the path of a better life and rebellion against Jesus will lead to destruction. Paul warns us that we must not think that because we are either Jew or Gentile that we will escape this. Throughout history there have been Jews who think by being Jewish they will inherit eternal life. In the same way, many Gentiles have believed the same about themselves only because they grew up in a Christian family. Neither of these heritages are enough to spare us from a lifestyle (and eternity) of destruction. Only personally accepting Jesus as our only means of access to God will save us.

THE LAW
2:12-29

Knowing the law does not make you a good citizen. Obeying the law is the only way to maintain a right standing in society. In the same way, knowing God's commands do not make you special—only obeying His commands grant us favor.

The law that Paul is talking about here is specifically the Jewish Law, or the commands given in the first five books of the Bible. The Law is a technical term in Judaism that refers to a set of enumerated commands developed from extrapolating from scripture the many explicit and inferred commands of God. The law can also be a less technical term that refers to the Old Testament as a whole.

Because this law was specifically given to the Hebrew people, Paul makes mention that its commands are actually quite universal. He tells us that Gentiles actually fulfill the law by nature even though they may be completely ignorant of its statutes. Our consciences witness to us the nature and requirements of God, whether we are Jew or Gentile.

Solomon spoke of this when he said;

> *He has made everything beautiful in its time.*
> *He has also set eternity in the human heart; yet*
> *no one can fathom what God has done from*
> *beginning to end.*

Ecclesiastes 3:11

Eternity has truly been written on the heart of every single person. Even though we may not have been born into a family that taught us the law, it is obvious to us somehow.

Paul has harsh things to say to the Jew who has grown up being taught the law but refuses to obey it. Just because a Jew knows the precepts and minutia of the law, does not mean that they obey it. He condemns those who study it and teach it only to fall short of it themselves.

Paul's harsh condemnation is not a rebuke of those who stumble into sin, but to those who contort and twist the law to bend it to their own predispositions toward sin. The Jewish leaders at this time were adept at making sure the way they interpreted the law always worked well for their pocketbooks and their lifestyles. Fornication, theft and cheating others were common in that day among the Jewish elite, but they exonerated themselves by making allowances within the law that made them look like special cases that the Lord was okay with.

This isn't a temptation that dwelt only within the Jewish elite. Every single person throughout history has a bent toward self-justification. We want to convince ourselves and others that the things we do are okay. We find ways to point to others around us who look worse than us so by comparison we look good. This is part of human nature, and it wars against the knowledge of God. The Pharisees of Paul's day and the politicians of ours are well-documented hypocrites who have had a track record of making sure that the laws they make and teach apply mostly to others.

Paul condemns the religious leaders of his day for stealing, committing adultery and cheating the Lord from their tithes. Paul even goes so far as to quote to them one of the most fear-invoking passages in scripture, Isaiah 52:5. Blaspheming God by their actions was the most serious of offenses.

It is common for people skilled in the law to twist it and contort it to make themselves look innocent. They may convince a court of law of their innocence, but those around them see through them. Their hypocrisy is evident to all, even though they may have convinced even themselves of their own innocence. We see this nearly every day from people in power, from our elected officials to Wall Street tycoons and even pastors of megachurches. The perks of being in charge have never been so good!

And they were good for the Jewish leaders in Paul's day as well, but he makes sure to warn them that they look every bit as greedy and wicked to the Gentiles as our leaders do today. Being circumcised and keeping a version of the law that suited them well did not make them pleasing to God.

Paul uses an interesting phrase to end this chapter. "Circumcision of the heart" is such a strange phrase. Circumcision was the surgical removal of the extra and unnecessary foreskin on male genitalia. From a religious perspective, it seems like such a strange thing, but God made a very big deal about it in the Old Testament. It didn't matter why God chose this as a law, it was only to be obeyed.

Paul makes it clear that circumcision was only an outward sign of something God wanted transformed within the hearts of His people. He wanted them to cut away the extra stuff from their person: the things that serve no purpose. Believing that how a man's genitals were treated as a baby is what made them good people was as crazy then as believing that we stand rightly before the Lord today because our parents and grandparents went to church.

We must all, Jew and Gentile, circumcise our hearts. We must cut away the things of this life that are unnecessary and often lead us away from God rather than to Him.

ROMANS CHAPTER 3

THE ADVANTAGE OF BEING A JEW
3:1-2

Paul has spent the last chapter breaking down any advantage Jews would think they have over Gentiles before God. He seems to have downplayed the value of physical circumcision and knowledge of the Law, but was that his intent?

Paul pivots now to look at things a little differently.

Paul's point in the last chapter was not to say that being Jewish is of no value, but to make it clear that being Jewish is not what saves a person. We see now that Paul is going to speak of the great value of being Jewish.

God chose and entrusted to the Jewish people His very Word. We should be eternally grateful to them that we are, as we will find out later, a wild olive branch that has been grafted into this family. Our savior is a Jewish man, and we should never forget that.

SAVED BY GRACE OR ADHERENCE?
3:3-8

Paul now begins what seems like an argument with himself. It seems like Paul is using a line of reasoning he has encountered along his travels. This shouldn't be too surprising to us, because these arguments have been thrown around over and over again for the past couple thousand years.

This idea that we should do evil since God gets the glory for providing us grace seems to be a very common idea today. Of course, it is never packaged quite that clearly, but it is ever-present today. There probably haven't been too many moments in the past two thousand years where some form of this thinking hasn't existed.

Paul makes it clear that if we think this, we are condemned before God and that we justly deserve it. We are condemned because this is a dangerous heresy and a rejection of the true gospel. Anyone who can justify doing evil because they think God is unjust in condemning us, knowing we're weak sinners, does not have the truth within them.

God does know that we are weak and prone to falling away. He has incredibly tender grace for us, but encouraging others to sin to magnify God's grace is a perversion of that grace and the nature of God.

Sadly, there are many stories today of young men and women struggling with lust who are counseled by their pastors and youth leaders just to engage in protected sex and repent later. Far too many counsel people to take the easy road and then trust that God will forgive them. This is a heretical perversion of God's grace.

Just because God is gracious and kind with us, does not mean that we should take sin lightly. Paul has just spent the last chapter warning those who think that because they know the Law they are free from God's wrath to be cautious in their thinking.

Paul speaks of those who slandered him by saying that he taught this very thing. At the time, the Pharisees taught that people must obey the Law completely to be justified before God. They had all but written out of their practice the necessity for the ongoing sacrifices at the Temple. They were using the Law, and especially their flawed interpretation of it, to justify themselves rather than relying on the grace of God.

It was probably these same people who were saying that Paul was teaching people just to sin as much as they want and ask for forgiveness later. This same overreaction to legalism has been echoed throughout history.

What makes this more challenging to comprehend, is that many people have taught that people were saved in the Old Testament by obedience to the Law and in the New Testament by grace. Nothing could be further from the truth. Paul teaches us that every single person is only saved by grace; in the Old Testament and in the New Testament. The book of Hebrews echoes this very clearly.

This is the essence of what Paul is conveying: Jew and Gentile are saved by the same grace; past, present and future.

NOT EVEN ONE
3:9-20

Paul references several Psalms that reiterate his point. He recites for us parts of Psalms 14, 53, 5 and 140 to show that we all are sinners; Jew and Gentiles. It is not through obedience that we can be saved, because every single one of us is a sinner.

Paul uses these Psalms to prove to those slanderers—those Pharisees and teachers of the Law who try to justify themselves by the Law—that the very Law they teach condemns them as someone who is unrighteous and doesn't even have it in their heart to truly seek God. These verses should silence the voice of every single person who thinks they can justify themselves.

Paul makes it abundantly clear that no one will be able to justify themselves by their adherence to the

Law, but this is exactly what so many Jewish Rabbis taught at the time.

This might make us think that the Law, then, is of no value. Many today say that the Law of God is something that has no bearing on the lives of New Testament believers. They say this mainly because of the mistaken belief that the people in the Old Testament were justified by the Law.

What Paul says instead is that the value of the Law is to make us aware that we are sinners. The Law proclaims to each of us that we are not righteous in God's sight. It proves to us now, and to the people in the Old Testament, that we are justly deserving punishment from God. The Law cannot make us clean, it can only make us guilty.

THE LAW AND FAITH
3:21-26

Paul now makes one of the most famous statements in Romans, that "all have sinned and fall short of the glory of God" (23). He makes this point because he says that the Law itself, and the Prophets of the Old Testament, testified that it was through the Messiah that we would be made right with God—not by our obedience to the Law.

Because Jesus shed His holy and righteous blood for us, we can now be saved. Paul tells us that up until the time of Jesus, the sins that had been committed were left unpunished. All creation was waiting for the arrival of the Son of God to come and take away our sins. Now that Jesus has been revealed, our acceptance or denial of Jesus is critically important. John puts it this way in his gospel:

> *Whoever believes in the Son has eternal life, but whoever rejects the Son will not see life, for God's wrath remains on them.*
>
> *John 3:36*

Because adherence to the Law isn't what saves us, we can't claim our own piety as a source of salvation. This cuts off self-justification that all humanity so desperately clings to. As Paul has just quoted, "we have all sinned;" Jew and Gentile.

SELF-JUSTIFICATION
3:21-26

What Paul calls boasting, we are calling self-justification. It was common for the religious leaders of Paul's day to "boast" about how righteous they were. Jesus told this parable:

> *To some who were confident of their own righteousness and looked down on everyone else, Jesus told this parable: "Two men went up to the temple to pray, one a Pharisee and the other a tax collector. The Pharisee stood by himself and prayed: 'God, I thank you that I am not like other people—robbers, evildoers, adulterers—or even like this tax collector. I fast twice a week and give a tenth of all I get.'*
>
> *"But the tax collector stood at a distance. He would not even look up to heaven, but beat his*

breast and said, 'God, have mercy on me, a sinner.'

"I tell you that this man, rather than the other, went home justified before God. For all those who exalt themselves will be humbled, and those who humble themselves will be exalted."

Luke 18:9-14

Humility is what is required to draw near to God. Without the humility where we acknowledge Jesus for our salvation and justification, we cannot be saved.

It has always required faith to be justified by God, in the Old and New Testament, so we have no claim to boasting about our own righteousness. That boasting is actually a sign that we have no salvation. It is a sign of our self-righteousness and self-justification.

Paul tells us that God is not the God of only the Jews, but the Gentiles also. He created all life on earth and He cares about every person. The Jews are special, as Paul will soon explain, not because they have kept the Law—because the Law was entrusted to them.

Don't forget to read Romans this week!
Visit 10WeekBible.com for more resources including daily podcasts, videos and more.

3

ROMANS 4-5

STUDY QUESTIONS

1. How does Christian faith differ from "Hallmark Christianity?"

2. Why was it important for Jews to be obedient to God in the Old Testament? Is it important to be obedient today?

3. Who are Abraham's children? What makes someone a child of Abraham, according to Paul (and Jesus)?

4. Why would Christians want to embrace suffering?

5. Do you believe that if God loves you, you will only succeed in life? Do you want to embrace suffering? Why or why not?

6. Before we accepted Jesus, what did we deserve? After accepting Jesus, what do we receive?

7. What is the difference between Adam's sin and Jesus' sacrifice?

8. What is the value and place of the Law? Why is the Law necessary for us to understand and accept Jesus' grace?

COMMENTARY NOTES

ROMANS CHAPTER 4

FAITH
4:1-8

Continuing what Paul was saying in chapter three, he turns our attention to Abraham. Abraham's righteousness, in the Old Testament, was not from his adherence to God's Law, but from his trust in God.

Abram believed the Lord, and he credited it to him as righteousness.

Genesis 15:6

Throughout Romans, Paul will make it abundantly clear that no one has ever been justified by their works. Unfortunately, this is still just as a prevalent an idea as it was in Paul's day. Far too many people believe they must do enough good to outweigh the bad to get into heaven.

We can refer to this as "Hallmark Christianity." These notions of doing enough good so that Saint Peter will weigh your actions on scales to decide whether to let you into heaven make for good cartoons and greeting cards, but they are absolutely incorrect.

The pagan Eastern philosophy of Karma is much the same. If we do enough good, good things will come to us; and likewise, if we do enough bad, bad things will happen to us. There is no place in the Bible, Old Testament or New, where we can find this kind of theology, but it remains an ever-present reality in the church today.

The Pharisees in Paul's day taught this kind of theology because it served them very well. For many dark years, this served the church clergy as well. If you are the teacher of God's Word to others, especially to a mostly illiterate people without direct access to the Bible, you can be the arbiter of what is right and wrong. All too often, men in this position of power have twisted God's Word to suit themselves.

Paul likens this to a wage-earner. If you work for someone, there is an agreement, either written or implied, that you deserve money for your hard work. The implication here is that if you work hard, you get paid, and if you mess up, you also reap the negative consequences of that too. You are due the compensation for what you have done, good or bad. It's "work Karma."

But if you haven't worked, and the master gives you money as a gift, it is not tied to what you have done or accomplished. In that way, nothing can be taken away from you for messing up an assignment you haven't even been given. God's grace cannot be earned by our works—only accepted as a gift.

We are not justified by our works, because we are all sinful. We are justified by God's gift, saved through our faith that He forgives our sins. Paul quotes where David said this same thing in the Old Testament, again pointing to the fact that no one has ever been saved through obedience.

OBEDIENCE
4:9-12

One of the main distinctions between the Jews and Gentiles of Paul's day was whether or not they were circumcised. The religious leaders taught that only the circumcised could know God because they were the ones walking in obedience.

It is true that the Jews were being obedient to God by being circumcised, but the fact that Jewish babies were circumcised had nothing to do with their salvation or standing with God.

We learn here that Abraham's righteousness by faith was actually granted before God told him to be circumcised. Circumcision was given as a sign and seal of that salvation and righteousness, not as the precursor to it. In that way, obedience isn't without importance. To the contrary, it is very important! What it is, however, is unnecessary for salvation.

Obedience is a logical response to the greatness of our salvation. It is the sign and seal that we have been granted righteousness and forgiveness of sins. It is the outward display of our gratitude for God not treating us as our sins deserve.

Abraham then becomes the father of not only the Jews, but of everyone with faith that the One True God will forgive our sins and grant us eternal life. The righteousness that we strive for has nothing to do with our obedience to circumcision or any other requirement, except the requirement to believe that God is who He says He is and that He will do for us what He says He will do.

ABRAHAM'S OFFSPRING
4:13-25

The promises of being a son or daughter of Abraham were, and still are, very important to the Jews. One of the ways in which the teaching of that inheritance was distorted in Paul's day was that only those who abided by the Law were Abraham's true descendants. We see this conflict take place between Jesus and the Pharisees:

To the Jews who had believed him, Jesus said, "If you hold to my teaching, you are really my disciples. Then you will know the truth, and the truth will set you free."

They answered him, "We are Abraham's descendants and have never been slaves of anyone. How can you say that we shall be set free?"

Jesus replied, "Very truly I tell you, everyone who sins is a slave to sin. Now a slave has no permanent place in the family, but a son belongs to it forever. So if the Son sets you free, you will be free indeed. I know that you are Abraham's descendants. Yet you are looking for a way to kill me, because you have no room for my word. I am telling you what I have seen in the Father's presence, and you are doing what you have heard from your father. "

"Abraham is our father," they answered.

"If you were Abraham's children," said Jesus, "then you would do what Abraham did. As it is,

34

you are looking for a way to kill me, a man who has told you the truth that I heard from God. Abraham did not do such things. You are doing the works of your own father."

"We are not illegitimate children," they protested. "The only Father we have is God himself."

Jesus said to them, "If God were your Father, you would love me, for I have come here from God. I have not come on my own; God sent me. Why is my language not clear to you? Because you are unable to hear what I say. You belong to your father, the devil, and you want to carry out your father's desires. He was a murderer from the beginning, not holding to the truth, for there is no truth in him. When he lies, he speaks his native language, for he is a liar and the father of lies. Yet because I tell the truth, you do not believe me! Can any of you prove me guilty of sin? If I am telling the truth, why don't you believe me? Whoever belongs to God hears what God says. The reason you do not hear is that you do not belong to God."

John 8:31-47

Jesus went so far as to say that those who try to justify themselves by their adherence to the Law are not, in fact, decedents of Abraham. He told the Jewish leaders that in this way, they were actually children of the devil!

Jesus' words must have been intolerably offensive to them, especially since He pointed out that they wanted to kill Him, an act of obedience to their true father.

In the same way, Paul makes it clear here in Romans

that there are only penalties and wrath found in the Law, but there is freedom in the forgiveness and gift of grace from Jesus. Jesus made it clear that natural birthright was not what makes us "children of Abraham," but our acceptance of the same faith that Abraham had. In that way, it doesn't matter whether we are Jews or Gentiles; we can all be Abraham's children and inherit his promises.

Paul concludes this thought by speaking about the faith of Abraham and Sarah that God would provide them a child in their old age. This may sound strange to many ears, because Sarah giving Hagar to Abraham to produce a child sounds like the very opposite of faith.

It was certainly a low point for the two of them, but it is clear that neither of them wavered in their faith. What is clear was that after some considerable delay, they thought that maybe God had left it up to them to fulfill this important promise. After all, the act of creating offspring isn't involuntary, so they took it upon themselves to find a way to fulfill God's promise.

This wasn't the best decision, but it was still done in faith! Because of that faith, God even promised to bless the offspring of Hagar in the same way; that He would make Ishmael into a great nation and people. But the promises God had intended were not to be inherited by Hagar's descendants, but by Sarah's.

How often do the same thing? Without wavering in our faith, we grow weary of waiting and take it upon ourselves to "help" God get the job done.

ROMANS CHAPTER 5

SUFFERING
5:1-5

Paul starts this chapter so well. Being justified by faith, rather than by works, is the most amazing reality of Christianity, but Paul goes off the rails almost immediately. After saying that our boast should be in the hope of God's glory instead of our own works, he brings in suffering.

Why does Paul want us to "glory in our sufferings?" He is working backwards from faith, which is the thing that we need to walk with God. Paul explains that faith is produced by hope, which in turn springs from character. Character is built through perseverance, and perseverance is derived through those sufferings.

Suffering is not the only thing that can eventually produce faith, but think about how many people you know who decided to turn their life over to Jesus because of how wonderful their life was going. How many people, because of their great wealth, all of a sudden, had an epiphany of God's goodness? It's definitely possible, but can you think of anyone it's ever happened to?

Think about your own life. When were the times that you turned the most intently to God? Were those times when you were so blown away by all of your prosperity that you just had to throw up your hands and worship God, or when you had gotten so desperate that you didn't know where else to turn?

Suffering, as it turns out, is the precursor to much of our life in God, and for that we should most definitely glory in it. Without that suffering, very seldom do we turn our hearts to Him. No one likes it, but it is almost always necessary.

One of the greatest sins of the modern "prosperity gospel" is not the notion that God wants us prosperous, but that it eliminates all notion of suffering. There are too many passages of scripture that make it abundantly clear that God really enjoys it when we prosper. In fact, He is setting us up to be incomprehensibly prosperous for all eternity. If His eternal city's streets are made of gold, what are our houses made of?

God isn't against nice things, and the prosperity gospel isn't wrong about that. But it equates material wealth with gaining God's love and approval. In many of its forms, it teaches that if you're rich, you're doing something right before the Lord. This is exactly the same error that the Pharisees of Paul's day made. It is very often just the opposite. Because of God's jealous love for us, He will send us trouble that will soften our hard hearts to Him.

Wealth, prosperity and comfort are truly blessings from God, but they can often be the very things that harden our hearts to Him. Suffering is of great value to every Christian, although it's not something we should go looking for. If our hearts are aimed at God, and He feels we need it to further refine us, suffering will find us.

RECONCILIATION
5:6-11

We did not buy our salvation with our prosperity. We couldn't purchase it with out influence. We are eternally helpless to save ourselves, as we have seen so far in Romans. Paul tells us that "at just the right time, when we were still powerless, Christ died for the ungodly." (v6).

Through His righteous blood, Jesus reconciled us to God. Even though we were steeped in our sin and rebellion against God, He showed His great love by dying for us. Without first seeing if we were going to respond to Him, Jesus died for us. Without precondition, He died. God's righteous wrath was on us, and now we can be free from it, and it had nothing to do with our own righteousness or ability.

Paul tells us that before Jesus, we were God's enemies, but because of Jesus' death we may be at peace with God. Paul doesn't stop there, however. Because Jesus has not only died, but risen from the dead, the deal that God has given us is truly mind-blowing. Instead of receiving God's wrath, we will receive His friendship, sonship and we will inherit the kingdom of heaven! Jesus has not only redeemed us to God, but He has granted us so much more for all eternity. Just look at some of the things He has promised us:

Whoever has ears, let them hear what the Spirit says to the churches. To the one who is victorious, I will give the right to eat from the tree of life, which is in the paradise of God...

...will not be hurt at all by the second death...

...I will also give that person a white stone with a new name written on it, known only to the one who receives it...

...I will give authority over the nations—that one 'will rule them with an iron scepter and will dash them to pieces like pottery'—just as I have received authority from my Father. I will also give that one the morning star...

...be dressed in white. I will never blot out the name of that person from the book of life, but will acknowledge that name before my Father and his angels...

...I will make a pillar in the temple of my God. Never again will they leave it. I will write on them the name of my God and the name of the city of my God, the new Jerusalem, which is coming down out of heaven from my God; and I will also write on them my new name...

...I will give the right to sit with me on my throne, just as I was victorious and sat down with my Father on his throne.

Revelation 2:7,11,17,26-28 & 3:5,12,21

We deserved eternal punishment for our sins, but because of Jesus, we not only get to avoid that (which is huge), but we also inherit all these incredible eternal promises! When we think about this, "good news" doesn't seem to do justice to the deal we have from God.

DEATH AND LIFE
5:12-19

We were hopeless to be saved by our adherence to the Law. Paul says that sin existed before the Law, but that there were no charges against anyone until it was spoken. Even still, death reigned over everyone from Adam until Moses, when the Law was given. Why? Even without the Law, we all fell short of God's glory, the glory He requires to be in His presence.

The Law was given to make us aware of that sin nature within us. It was given to illuminate to us the terrible state we were in. The Law was given to point us toward grace. Unlike the sin and death that reigned in us, however, our salvation is much greater. One sin doomed all humanity. One man's actions broke our immortality and caused us to be enemies of God.

Paul tells us that even though one sin condemned humanity, we have something greater at work within us now. Jesus' righteous blood and His resurrection from the dead have offered us, and to everyone who chooses to believe, the hope of glory that He promises in the passages of Revelation listed earlier.

Paul says that Jesus' sacrifice is incomparable to Adam's sin. For Adam's and our sin, we justly deserve eternal punishment. For Jesus' blood, we are offered so much more than just salvation from hell. We have literally been given thrones to rule with Jesus! When Paul says that Adam's sin and Jesus' gift to us cannot be compared, it may just be the understatement of eternity!

SIN AND GRACE
5:20-21

Paul tells us that the Law was not given to us to help us achieve our salvation, but to make it abundantly clear just how fall we have fallen short of the glory of God. The Law actually gives sin a name. Because of the Law, we know exactly what is wrong in our hearts. It points out and illuminates for us the very negative reality that faces each one of us.

The Law actually had the effect of increasing sin in us. Before we know we're breaking a rule, we're less likely to try to break it. Once we know what that rule is, something within us causes us to want to actually try to break it. Far from giving us a path to be justified before God, the Law actually increases our sin.

This is what Paul says makes God's grace so much more powerful. When He laid out His righteous standards for us, it actually caused us to want to break them even more. Paul has already told us that even Gentiles who never had the Law obeyed it because it was obvious from nature. Adam's sin planted something so deviant within us that we seek out sin when we know its name.

God's grace is that much more powerful in nature then, because when we doubled-down on our own rebellion, that's when Jesus gave Himself up for us. His grace is truly magnified when we think of our propensity and desire to sin. It wasn't for people who were really trying to be better that Jesus sacrificed Himself for, but for those who were actively trying to find ways to break the Law and sin.

Don't forget to read Romans this week!
Visit 10WeekBible.com for more resources including daily podcasts, videos and more.

ROMANS 6-7

STUDY QUESTIONS

1. Why do you think Paul tells us to die like Jesus? Is that something you honestly want to do?

2. What is God's grace for in our lives?

3. What does Paul say our human limitations are?

4. What are Paul's two metaphors in chapter six? Why do you think he uses these?

5. Is the Law good or bad for us? Why?

6. If you have accepted Jesus, are you free to sin as much as you want? Why or why not?

7. How is our relationship to the Law like an addict's relationship to drugs? How can we overcome?

COMMENTARY NOTES

ROMANS CHAPTER 6

FREEDOM FROM SIN
6:1-14

Who knows someone asking to die a death like Jesus? Does anyone you know want to die on a cross? It was an excruciating death that was a travesty anyone ever had to suffer. The ancient Romans were masters of torture on a level the world has seldom seen.

So why would Paul want Christians to seek to die like Jesus? Why would we want to be buried with Him? This chapter should create a wealth of questions within us as we seek to understand what God is speaking to us through Paul's words here.

One of the fundamental aspects of our humanity is that we have a bias for life. When a lifeguard tries to save a drowning person, the first rule is that they must always physically subdue them. Why? Because the drowning person is fighting for their life, and that response is so innate within them that when the lifeguard shows up, they cannot tell the difference between the person saving them and the water that is killing them. They will actually fight the person saving them and both may drown.

If our bias is geared so much toward living, why is Paul asking us to die? Didn't Jesus die for us?

Paul wants us to know the very real situation we face. It is easy in our efforts to self-justify, as he has already made plain, that we can turn a very blind eye to the nature of sin in our lives.

Paul tells the Romans that the water baptism they received as believers is there to remind them that they have figuratively died with Christ so that they may also be raised to new life, not so figuratively, just like Jesus was. What we and the Roman believers died from was sin, and we have been raised to a new life, free from the slavery of sin.

Paul uses these two metaphors, death and slavery, to make his point clear that sin is a big deal, and that the fact we have been saved from it is an even bigger deal. Before we accepted Jesus, we were slaves to sin, helpless to escape its clutches. By choosing to "die" with Jesus, we allow that enslaved man or woman to die because of the promise of resurrection.

The reality of the resurrection was so real to Paul that he had no problem asking people to die with Christ. Our bias toward self-preservation is easily resolved in his mind by the overcoming power of Jesus to join us into the same resurrection He had.

Death only has one opportunity on our lives. A dead person cannot die more. So if death is final, then the resurrection Jesus offers us is as well. That is the point that Paul makes in this passage: that choosing death to sin is a final decision, and the result is everlasting freedom from sin and eternal life.

Paul is speaking half-metaphorically. He is not asking for people to literally commit suicide and then experience physical resurrection. No, Paul is asking us to understand that because physical resurrection is such an important reality, we see ourselves as figuratively already dead to sin. Sin is that big a deal that Paul wants us to view ourselves as having died to it.

He finishes these two metaphors of slavery and death by reminding us that we must not let sin reign in our bodies. Sin is always available to us. Paul wants us to take the hard-lined mindset that it isn't. It's not that we cannot still choose to sin, but that we see ourselves as already dead and resurrected so that sin is no longer the driving force in our lives.

ALLEGIANCE
6:15-18

Paul makes it very clear that the freedom we have received in Jesus is not the freedom to sin, but exactly the opposite. The testimony of scripture tells us that before the salvation of Jesus, it is difficult, at best, to avoid the temptation to sin. Paul goes even so far as to say that we are so bound to it before Jesus that we are slaves to it, lacking the freedom to disobey its commands.

The grace Jesus gives us, then, is to choose not to sin. It is a common idea, both now and throughout history, to view the freedom Jesus has given us as a "get out of hell free card" that gives us license to dabble more with sin. Paul wants us to know that nothing could be further from the truth.

Paul doubles back to his slavery metaphor to say

that we have exchanged one master for another: we were slaves to sin, but now we are slaves to righteousness through Jesus. In doing so, he uses a very important word: allegiance.

We have pledged our allegiance to the pattern of teaching that Jesus has given us and that Paul is reiterating. His figurative speech in this chapter is summed up by this word. We have willingly pledged our allegiance to Jesus, and we must no longer split our allegiance between Him and sin. We cannot serve two masters, as Jesus told us. We are now slaves not only to Jesus, but to the righteousness that comes from following Him.

Many today believe that teaching adherence to righteousness is the opposite of the grace that Paul teaches in Romans, but nothing could be further from the truth. Teaching people to be good and righteous enough to earn their way to God is the antithesis of what Paul is teaching in Romans. Teaching people that because of Jesus' salvation, we must put off sin and embrace righteous living is the very heart of Romans.

The law only further enslaves us to sin, so we cannot earn our salvation by trying to be righteous. That enslavement precludes us from actually doing the things necessary to live righteously in the first place. Grace frees us from the enslavement of the law of sin, giving us our first true opportunity to live righteously, but we only have that opportunity because of the sacrifice of Jesus.

Righteousness is at the center of this book and properly understanding how and why we choose to walk in it is the substance of what Paul wants us to learn. Righteous acts done to earn God's forgiveness earn us punishment; righteous acts done in response to God's forgiveness earn us a reward.

HUMAN LIMITATIONS
6:19-23

Paul tells us he has been speaking to us this way because of our human limitations. That is a kind way of saying that we are all a little dull an not quite bright enough to realize what's actually going on, and he was no exception.

Paul believed that he was earning his place to stand before God by persecuting the very people who were telling him of the free gift of God's grace. As Paul persecuted Christians, he thought he was attaining the righteousness that God required. Instead, God told him he was actually fighting directly against the one he thought he was offering righteousness to.

Unfortunately, Paul's story is also ours. Our human limitation is that our eyes are clouded by sin. Self-justification becomes our default, and in doing so, we rewrite our own laws to suit our manner of living and we call it righteousness. Self-justification will never equal righteousness, and we will never find our way to God through it, but it is the first way people try to relate to God.

By using the metaphors he has in this chapter, Paul is figuratively trying to grab us and shake us hard enough to wake us up from the deception we have so easily believed in. Death and slavery are very bold and extreme metaphors, and Paul uses them as hyperbole to show us just how hard it is for us to wrap our minds around the idea of grace.

To this day, Romans itself is used as a proof-text for every kind of wayward teaching about grace, reinforcing what Paul is saying about our limitation. Some argue that unless we act in perfect righteousness, never sinning, we cannot receive salvation. Others teach that because Jesus has saved us, we are free to sin as much as we want without consequence. Both are exactly what Paul argues against, but because it is so hard for us to understand grace rightly, opposite extremes to what Paul teaches persist.

Paul concludes this thought by one more time telling us that it is only because we are "slaves" to God that we even have the ability to live holy. Righteousness is not the way to God, but instead the only acceptable lifestyle after we have received the grace of God.

ROMANS CHAPTER 7

DEATH CHANGES THINGS
7:1-6

Lots of things change when people die. As Paul points out, it is really difficult to prosecute a dead person. The laws that applied to them while they were alive just don't seem to carry as much weight once they've been buried.

Police are actually trained not to kill people in a gunfight if at all possible. As it turns out, victims never feel a sense of justice unless they can see that person stand trial for themselves. Even if police feel justified to kill a person shooting back at or fighting with them, they are taught to restrain themselves for the sake of the victims. A dead man cannot stand trial.

Paul tells us that it is the same way with sin. He uses this death analogy with a woman in marriage. Then and now we make vows to the effect of "'till death do us part." When a husband dies, a woman is free to remarry as she chooses, but if she crosses those lines before her husband dies, there are no shortage of words to describe her.

Sadly, that analogy doesn't work as well the other way around, but the point is clear: death sets us free from the law. If we die to sin and the law, we can be set free from its punishments.

Paul has nearly beaten the death analogy to…death, but it is important for us to understand what he is conveying if we are to come away from Romans with the right understanding.

Is The Law Bad?
7:7-13

Paul makes it abundantly clear in Romans that the Law is actually pure and holy, given to us by God. At the same time, he makes it clear that the Law actually multiplies sin within us. That is a paradoxical reality that causes many, if not most, readers of Romans to truly struggle.

How can the Law be holy and at the same time be the thing that increases sin within us? It may sound contradictory, but when we look at ourselves through the lens of human nature, it begins to make perfect sense.

LEARNING FROM ADDICTS

Many drug addicts understand this very well. When they started using drugs, many users felt in control and very self-righteous. They think of themselves as being better than all those other people who get hooked. They know better and they will do better because they are better, or so they think. They begin with a feeling of control, but as they dive deeper into the belly of the beast they have paired themselves to, they realize they have lost control.

For many drug addicts, the law gets quite literally involved. Many times it is the consequences of the Law that gives them pause enough to look at their life and realize that it had spun out of control. Many drug addicts will tell you that they thank God for their drug addiction, because except for it, they would not have known how utterly broken they truly were.

Their drug addiction exposed the reality that was present in them before they ever began using: they were lost. Like Paul says here in chapter seven, their addiction, seizing its opportunity, produced every kind of destruction in their life. It was actually the thing that opened their eyes to how lost they were at the outset. An addict's problem is that they don't know on the front end how lost they are until they are so deep into drug abuse that they don't know what to do to get out.

It is their addiction, as bad as it is, that opens the eyes of an addict to the reality of who they have been all along. The Law is the same way. Until we are confronted with the true nature of our rebellion, we are all blind to it. The Law affords us the opportunity to see ourselves as we truly are: sinners separated from God. It is not God who causes us to sin, but our rebellion against the Law. As Paul says, the Law is "holy, righteous and good" (v12).

THE PROBLEM IS WITH ME
7:14-25

It has become quite en vogue in recent years to teach people that Paul says the Law is evil. Often, Romans is used as the prooftext. Paul unequivocally says the opposite, but this is nothing new but a repackaging of ancient heresies that have been long refuted. The modern trend stems from the idea that the "Old Testament God" is not good, therefore the Law must be bad too.

The problem, as we have seen, is not with the Law, but with us. It is our own sinful desires within us that drive us to rebel against the Law. The Law proves to us that we are not as good as we think we are. It exposes us. The better we know the Law, the more it exposes within us our own rebellion and sinful nature. It is the very thing that shows us we need freedom. Without it, we would continue in our own self-righteous, self-justifying ways.

Paul is like all of us. We know that we want to do good, but we find being bad so much easier. Like Paul, our souls cry out for freedom from this "wretched" person that we are.

There is a better way, but it requires as much slavish devotion to something new as did our sin require slavish devotion to fulfilling every lustful desire to ourselves.

It requires slavish devotion to Jesus.

Don't forget to read Romans this week!
Visit 10WeekBible.com for more resources including daily podcasts, videos and more.

ROMANS 8

STUDY QUESTIONS

1. What does it take to live without condemnation? Do you feel like you live free from condemnation?

2. What does it take to please God? Do you feel like you please God with your life? Why or why not?

3. What does Paul say our primary hope should be? Do you feel like that is your primary hope? If it's not, what can you do to change?

4. What value does Paul place on eternity? Do you feel like eternity means as much to you as Paul? Would you be willing to suffer like Paul in light of eternity?

5. What is predestination?

6. How do you think that God predestines us? Do you struggle with understanding it?

7. What are the things that God has helped you become a conquerer of because of Jesus? Do you feel like a conquerer most of the time, or a failure? What can you do to change that?

COMMENTARY NOTES

ROMANS CHAPTER 8

NO CONDEMNATION
8:1-4

We can live free of the condemnation that comes from the Law at work in our lives. As we feel the weight of sin, shame and the testimony of the Law in our lives, we have two options: we can double down into our self-justification, or we can surrender.

That surrender looks a lot like the death that Paul has been talking about. Being "in" Christ Jesus, as Paul explains, is the thing that sets us free and actually gives us life. If we are going to join ourselves to Christ, it means we must renounce the things of this world.

To give up things that our body has grown accustomed to is painful. Consider again a drug addict—the pain and torment of giving up drugs can feel like death to them. Their body actually thinks it needs the drugs it has been continually fed. In the same way, our sinful desires become a drug to our flesh. Our bodies believe they need those sinful indulgences, and to give them up feels like death.

Paul's metaphor grows stronger the older we get and the deeper into sin we dive. Children that come to faith at a young age do not have to experience that feeling of death, but many unbelievers have looked at the prospects of having to give up their sin to become

Christians with great turmoil. The truth is that we cannot leave sin behind and then follow Jesus, but the other way around. Jesus gives us the power to leave our sin behind. The death we fear, under the power of the Holy Spirit, quickly becomes nothing to us.

Paul's death metaphor only feels like death on the front end. After we have accepted Jesus and the Holy Spirit indwells us, we actually experience true freedom for the first time. That is when we realize the powerlessness of the law. It gave us no ability to live free from sin, it only made us aware it existed. Life in the Spirit, as Paul describes it, is the truest freedom we have as humans.

PLEASING GOD
8:5-8

Children often wonder how they can please their parents. It may not be the primary preoccupation of a child's mind, but it can be a daunting one, especially if there is not an active and thriving relationship there. How many people in our world suffer from wondering if they please their father, or worse yet, have to live with the knowledge that their father is actually displeased with them?

One of the pains of human existence is living in the tension of not knowing if there is a God out there, and whether or not we have the ability to please Him. One of the primary reasons people throw themselves into lives of sin is to drown out the pain from unanswered questions like those. Many people never experience the liberty to fully think through questions like that because of the earthly trouble they encounter, further compounding the condemnation they feel. In these ways, the mind "governed by the flesh" (v6) truly is death.

Not every believer experiences perfect peace, but compared to those who are dying in the flesh, it is a night and day difference. That is because, as Paul says, if you live in the flesh, it is impossible to please God. That deep nagging and gnawing sense that so many people live with is a deep human instinct God gave us to draw us to Himself. The Holy Spirit testifies to us that we lack something important.

In the same way, Paul will soon explain that for those who follow God, the Spirit also "himself testifies with our spirit that we are God's children" (v16).

THE SPIRIT OF ADOPTION
8:9-17

As Christians, our primary hope cannot be that we will have a comfortable life. It cannot be that we will have enough money and food to provide for ourselves and our families. It cannot be that we will one day own a home, two cars and have two and a half children. Although the Lord does enjoy it when His people prosper, these are all a far cry from the great hope we long for.

That great hope is that one day Jesus will return and bring our world into perfect justice and peace. Our great hope is that because of Jesus' shed blood, our sins have been forgiven and we will spend eternity with Him.

Paul tells us that our bodies are still subject to death because of sin, but that there is something that awaits us. The Holy Spirit will grant us life because of the righteousness of Jesus. Eternal life is our great reward; nothing else in this life compares to that one hope.

The greatest question, and the greatest longing we have as believers, is how can we live pleasing before the Lord. Paul tells us that if we have accepted Jesus, then we have the Spirit living within us. That Spirit gives us the ability to cry out, just like Jesus did, to our Daddy. Pleasing God is no longer an issue for those of us, as Paul says, who have experienced the adoption as sons and daughters to God. We are now the ones with perfect access to Him.

While humanity lives for itself in the flesh, it struggles with its identity before God, completely unable to please Him. As Christians, we no longer have to please Him, because our presence is pleasing to Him.

Paul transitions from the joy and pleasure of our adoption into this family to remind us that if we share in the joy and glory of God, we must also share in his sufferings.

SUFFERING
8:18-27

When Paul says that his "present sufferings are not worth comparing with the glory that will be revealed in us" (v18) in eternity, we must consider what those sufferings he encountered were. Paul, during his life-time, suffered:

- A stoning, that he miraculously survived (2 Corinthians 11:25)
- Unjust imprisonment, for years (2 Corinthians 11:23, Acts 24:27)
- Multiple beatings with rods. (2 Corinthians 11:25)
- Ongoing slander (2 Corinthians 11:26)
- Losing many friends, multiple times (2 Timothy 4:10, 2 Timothy 1:15, 16)
- Multiple shipwrecks (2 Corinthians 11:25)
- Thirty-nine lashes. Five times! (2 Corinthians 11:24)

If these are some of the things that Paul suffered, we must take him very seriously when he says that our present suffering doesn't compare to what we will inherit. For most of us, this list will never be a reality in our lives.

Hebrews chapter 11 lists ancients of the faith who experienced pain and suffering, but who looked to a future they knew they would only inherit after their natural deaths. There is something about the life we will inherit forever that should change how we view reality now. It should change not only our thoughts, but our lives and lifestyle.

There is an old saying, "that person is so heavenly minded, they're of no earthly good." Paul says that of Christians, precisely the opposite is true. We are of the most earthly good when our hearts and minds are fixed squarely on eternity.

Even creation, the earth itself, yearns, groans and is frustrated to wait for the return of Jesus to usher in eternity. Paul tells us that as children of God, those of us who have the Spirit, we also groan for that day when Jesus returns to bring perfect peace and justice.

To understand this "blessed hope," as it is called, we must first understand hope. On multiple occasions, the New Testament mentions hope as the precursor to faith. Hope is always for something we do not currently have. Once we have something, there is no more need to hope because we are satisfied.

When people say things like "I hope nothing goes wrong today," they are not so much announcing something they have placed their hope in, as much as something they have anxiety about. True hope is never away from something bad but always toward something good,; something better, but something we do not yet have.

Hope transitions into faith when we begin to act upon that hope we have. When our hope begins to change our actions, that's what the Bible calls faith. Faith, as a Christian, is the alteration of our lifestyle once we realize the promises of our future. We do not currently walk in the perfect peace and justice of eternity, but our hope inspires faith, which causes us to live entirely differently now. Christians then, are not those with their "heads in the clouds," but the only people whose feet are truly planted on firm ground.

PREDESTINATION
8:28-30

Romans 8:28 is one of the most famous single verses in the Bible. It lays out a hope for us in this life, that all the things we suffer and go through have a purpose in God. It is only granted to those who love God, however. All things do not work together for those who have not "been called according to his purpose" (v28).

This leads us to investigate what "called" means. Paul quickly answers that with one of the most contentious and hotly debated ideas in Christian history: predestination.

This big word, depending on your theological stripe or denominational affiliation, carries a lot of baggage with it. It can mean anything from God's holy love for you; to an irresistible grace that means that God has chosen some and rejected others before they were even born.

Two of the primary theological perspectives on this topic are called Calvanism and Arminianism. Calvanism teaches that God has already selected those who will be saved and those who will be condemned to hell. Arminianism teaches that people are who decide whether or not they will follow God and receive eternal life or not.

These are gross over-simplifications of two theological systems developed and refined over centuries. In the end, they are trying to make sense of something incredibly difficult to understand.

David had this to say about this very topic:

You have searched me, Lord,
and you know me.
You know when I sit and when I rise;
you perceive my thoughts from afar.
You discern my going out and my lying down;
you are familiar with all my ways.
Before a word is on my tongue
you, Lord, know it completely.
You hem me in behind and before,
and you lay your hand upon me.
Such knowledge is too wonderful for me,
too lofty for me to attain.

Psalm 139:1-6

In this Psalm, David acknowledges that God knows everything he does before he does it, but that such knowledge is far too above David's head for him to understand. David may have been a shepherd, but he was no dummy. For centuries, a fight has raged among those who claim to be Calvanist verses those who hold to Arminian teachings, all in search of an understanding of something David said was too hard to understand.

David's understanding of the principle of predestination is a much better way for us to view this than either Calvanism or Arminianism. How God's sovereignty and foreknowledge work are not for us to comprehend, only to accept. But Paul also has a better way.

GOD IS FOR US
8:31-39

Paul would probably be appalled that this one phrase about predestination had been used for so much infighting and bitterness within the church for so long. Paul spends little time on the topic of predestination, but instead points us to the outcome of God's knowledge and sovereignty: that if He is for us, who can be against us?

Paul's question doesn't mean to eliminate the suffering we encounter at the hands of others, but to help us understand it in its proper context.

We serve the God who does things that are so far above our understanding, and He is on our side. Compared to that, what is suffering? What is it that people would come against us? What are any negatives we may encounter in life compared to having the one true God who is for us? He's on our side!

Paul quotes the Psalmist that we face death and suffering, but does not quote the next part, which says this:

Awake, Lord! Why do you sleep?

Rouse yourself! Do not reject us forever.

Why do you hide your face

and forget our misery and oppression?

We are brought down to the dust;

our bodies cling to the ground.

Rise up and help us;

rescue us because of your unfailing love.

Psalm 44:23-26

It seems clear that Paul intended the readers to understand the outcome of the prior quotation. Even though we suffer and seem to be headed to the slaughter, we know that there is a God who will save us because of His unfailing love.

Paul ends this passage with possibly the most poetic and beautiful of all the things he wrote in the New Testament. This passage is worthy of special attention and meditation, because it summarizes our reality, both now and forever.

> *No, in all these things we are more than conquerors through him who loved us. For I am convinced that neither death nor life, neither angels nor demons, neither the present nor the future, nor any powers, neither height nor depth, nor anything else in all creation, will be able to separate us from the love of God that is in Christ Jesus our Lord.*

Romans 8:37-39

Don't forget to read Romans this week!
Visit 10WeekBible.com for more resources including daily podcasts, videos and more.

6

ROMANS 9

STUDY QUESTIONS

1. Would you be willing to offer yourself to suffer God's wrath in exchange for someone else, like Paul does for the Israelites? Why or why not?

2. What do you think made Paul, an apostle to the Gentiles, so passionate about the Israelites?

3. Does Paul say the church has replaced Israel as God's chosen people? Explain.

4. What does God's foreknowledge have to do with the debate between Jews and Gentiles?

5. Does God only reward those who have followed Him their whole lives? What about people whose families have a Christian history?

6. Are Gentile Christians required to convert to Judaism to truly know God? Why are why not?

7. What do you think the value of being a Jew is? What is the value of being a Gentile?

Commentary Notes

Romans Chapter 9

Israel
9:1-5

Paul dramatically shifts gears as we turn our attention to his people, the Israelites. In a way, Paul is standing with one hand on the Bible and one hand in the air to swear that what he is saying is true. He has genuine anguish over the fact that the Jewish people had rejected Jesus as their Messiah, something that was already painfully clear by the time Paul wrote this.

One can only imagine the conversations Paul must have had with the Lord where he asked God to exchange them for him. Was he serious? Did he really ask God for it? If he did, was he prepared for the Lord to say "okay?"

Paul knows that what he wished wasn't possible, but it brings him no less grief to see God's chosen people reject the God who chose them. And again Paul reiterates that the Law and the covenants were holy instruments God gave to the Israelites, not unholy condemnation devices as so many teach today. Paul's heart is broken that his peoples' eyes have been darkened, just as his were, to the truth of Jesus.

One of the great ironies in life is that often the very things we say in favor of something get turned against us and used to justify the opposite of what we meant.

Paul's desire to see Israel saved is one such lament. Throughout the centuries, this passage, and many others, have been used to teach what is commonly referred to as "Replacement Theology."

Replacement Theology teaches that because the Jews rejected Jesus, God has rejected them, and all the promises given to Israel in the Old Testament have been transferred to the New Testament church, thereby replacing literal Israel with a "spiritual Israel" in the church. This is not only something Paul never says, it is exactly the opposite of his lament here.

He reaffirms that to them is traced the human ancestry to the Messiah as well as the blessing of all the law and prophets.

PHYSICAL AND SPIRITUAL DESCENDANTS
9:6-9

Paul's words are often twisted here as he describes children "of the promise" versus those natural descendants of Abraham. People use this passage to say that Israel has been rejected and instead God has chosen spiritual descendants who belong to Jesus, not Abraham.

Paul does not make that case here, and he will more soundly refute such a claim later when he speaks about being "grafted in" to the "tree" of the Lord. What Paul is saying here is that the literal, physical descendants of Abraham are not the only legitimate children of promise.

Paul is not transferring ownership of the promises of

God from one people to another, from Jews to Gentile Christians, but making the benefits of those promises more inclusive of both groups. Because of the blood of Jesus, Jews and Gentiles may both now inherit the promises of God. Before Jesus, to be a benefactor, one must have converted to Judaism by becoming circumcised and following all the laws and customs of Moses.

GENTILES V. ISRAELITES
9:10-18

In the end, God gets to choose how things in His created order work. We unfortunately, do not have such a privilege. As much as we may want to, we are not the arbiters of what is right and wrong. We do not get to negotiate the terms by which we are saved. Paul reminds us of several people from scripture that bear this out.

Pharaoh, Esau and Jacob all had their places in God's destiny for Israel. With these examples, Paul circles back around to the idea of predestination. This passage, like our previous ones, is used to justify the thought that we have no choice in the matter of whether or not we are saved.

The truth of God's sovereignty and foreknowledge cannot be overlooked in scripture, and Paul points that out clearly here. It is not up to us how God's kingdom works, but to him alone. We must choose whether or not we want to abide by His reality, or one of our own creation.

Paul does not, however, make it clear that we have

no choice in the matter. He does not settle the dispute between Calvanist and Arminian: he does just the opposite actually.

WHAT DOES IT MATTER THEN?
9:19-29

Paul creates a hypothetical argument to make the case between predestination and free will a little muddier. He imagines someone saying that God is unjust to blame us for our actions if He is solely responsible for them. The obvious response is that we do not have the right to argue with God, our creator, for how He has created His universe.

It would seem then that Paul is on the side of the Calvanists, until he begins to point out chosen passages from scripture. He quotes Hosea first, making it clear that God had chosen other people besides the Jews to call His people. In the days when it was blasphemy to say that anyone could come to God except through conversion to Judaism, Hosea says exactly that.

Then Hosea continues and tells us that God will treat those who are His people like they aren't. This again brings us back to the argument that God has rejected Israel in lieu of the Church, those saints He has preordained to receive eternal life. But again, nothing is quite that simple in this chapter. Paul doubles back around and makes it clear that also is not the case.

Isaiah 10 tells us that although many Israelites

would reject salvation, still a remnant of them would be left. This is not speaking of a "remnant" of Gentile believers, but of Jewish ones. All Israel will eventually inherit the promises of God on account of the few who remained faithful to Him throughout the ages.

Paul then quotes Isaiah chapter one and it becomes clear what he is saying. The election he is speaking of is not some irresistible grace for all believers (not in this passage, at least), His ability to fulfill His promises to the Jews and His prerogative to incorporate others into those promises as well. God is not going to cut off Israel as He did with Sodom and Gomorrah, but He will leave literal and physical descendants to inherit the promises.

God will also allow Gentile believers into the fold of God's sheep pen. Paul is answering Jewish reservations of this inclusive grace, much like in the parable Jesus told.

> "For the kingdom of heaven is like a landowner who went out early in the morning to hire workers for his vineyard. He agreed to pay them a denarius[a] for the day and sent them into his vineyard.
>
> "About nine in the morning he went out and saw others standing in the marketplace doing nothing. He told them, 'You also go and work in my vineyard, and I will pay you whatever is right.' So they went.
>
> "He went out again about noon and about three in the afternoon and did the same thing. About five in the afternoon he went out and found still

others standing around. He asked them, 'Why have you been standing here all day long doing nothing?'

"'Because no one has hired us,' they answered.

"He said to them, 'You also go and work in my vineyard.'

"When evening came, the owner of the vineyard said to his foreman, 'Call the workers and pay them their wages, beginning with the last ones hired and going on to the first.'

"The workers who were hired about five in the afternoon came and each received a denarius. So when those came who were hired first, they expected to receive more. But each one of them also received a denarius. When they received it, they began to grumble against the landowner. 'These who were hired last worked only one hour,' they said, 'and you have made them equal to us who have borne the burden of the work and the heat of the day.'

"But he answered one of them, 'I am not being unfair to you, friend. Didn't you agree to work for a denarius? Take your pay and go. I want to give the one who was hired last the same as I gave you. Don't I have the right to do what I want with my own money? Or are you envious because I am generous?'

"So the last will be first, and the first will be last."

Matthew 20:1-16

Jesus told this parable to make it clear that "others" who had not "worked" like the first would be allowed

75

into his kingdom. He was speaking about the Jewish objections to Gentiles being allowed in without first having to convert to Judaism. By His sovereign will, God chose to allow the Gentiles in.

This reality was reiterated, much to the chagrin of those Pharisees and teachers of the law who became Christians in the early church:

> *Then some of the believers who belonged to the party of the Pharisees stood up and said, "The Gentiles must be circumcised and required to keep the law of Moses."*
>
> *The apostles and elders met to consider this question. After much discussion, Peter got up and addressed them: "Brothers, you know that some time ago God made a choice among you that the Gentiles might hear from my lips the message of the gospel and believe. God, who knows the heart, showed that he accepted them by giving the Holy Spirit to them, just as he did to us. He did not discriminate between us and them, for he purified their hearts by faith. Now then, why do you try to test God by putting on the necks of Gentiles a yoke that neither we nor our ancestors have been able to bear? No! We believe it is through the grace of our Lord Jesus that we are saved, just as they are."*
>
> *The whole assembly became silent as they listened to Barnabas and Paul telling about the signs and wonders God had done among the Gentiles through them. When they finished, James spoke up. "Brothers," he said, "listen to me. Simon a has described to us how God first*

intervened to choose a people for his name from the Gentiles. The words of the prophets are in agreement with this, as it is written:

"'After this I will return

and rebuild David's fallen tent.

Its ruins I will rebuild,

and I will restore it,

that the rest of mankind may seek the Lord,

even all the Gentiles who bear my name,

says the Lord, who does these things' —

things known from long ago.

"It is my judgment, therefore, that we should not make it difficult for the Gentiles who are turning to God. Instead we should write to them, telling them to abstain from food polluted by idols, from sexual immorality, from the meat of strangled animals and from blood. For the law of Moses has been preached in every city from the earliest times and is read in the synagogues on every Sabbath."

Acts 15:5-21

GENTILES ALLOWED IN BY SOVEREIGN GRACE
9:30-33

Paul concludes this chapter by making clear that Gentiles have attained the same grace offered to Jews. They have received it not through adherence to the Law, as Paul calls a pursuit of righteousness here, but through a pursuit of faith.

In that way, Jesus truly fulfilled the prophecy of Him in Isaiah eight, that He was a stumbling block to those seeking the folly of self-justification through the Law. To the contrary, those who believe in Him will never receive the penalties of the Law that cannot justify.

They will inherit eternal life and never be put to shame.

Don't forget to read Romans this week!
Visit 10WeekBible.com for more resources including daily podcasts, videos and more.

ROMANS 10-11

STUDY QUESTIONS

1. Were the Jews' knowledge during Paul's day based on truth? In what ways do you think it is possible for you today to base your "knowledge" on falsehood, and how can you avoid it?

2. What was wrong with the Israelites' zeal in Paul's day?

3. How had the Israelites established their own right-eousness, and what are the ways we do the same today?

4. Why did it benefit Gentiles for Jews to reject Jesus? What will the benefit be to Gentiles when the Jews accept Jesus?

5. Why must Gentiles be careful how they think of themselves in relation to Jews?

6. How do you think a proper relationship between Jewish and Gentile Christians would look?

COMMENTARY NOTES

ROMANS CHAPTER 10

MY PRAYER TO GOD FOR ISRAEL
10:1-4

You can really hear Paul's anguish for his people as you read the words of this passage. He knew what it was like to be zealous without knowledge.

It's a funny thing how easy it is to gain incredible amounts of knowledge, only to find out that it is all wrong. Paul thought his persecution of the Christians would be accounted to him as true zeal for God. He probably thought about stories like when Moses commanded the Levites to take a sword and kill those who had defiled the Israelites at the base of Mount Sinai:

Moses saw that the people were running wild and that Aaron had let them get out of control and so become a laughingstock to their enemies. So he stood at the entrance to the camp and said, "Whoever is for the Lord, come to me." And all the Levites rallied to him.

Then he said to them, "This is what the Lord, the God of Israel, says: 'Each man strap a sword to his side. Go back and forth through the camp from one end to the other, each killing his brother and friend and neighbor.' " The Levites did as Moses commanded, and that day about three thousand of the people died. Then Moses said, "You have been set apart to the Lord today, for you were against your own sons and brothers, and he has blessed you this day."

Exodus 32:25-29

Or maybe he had been thinking of the time when Aaron's grandson, Phinehas, killed an Israelite man for sleeping with a foreign woman who was enticing him to worship idols:

Then an Israelite man brought into the camp a Midianite woman right before the eyes of Moses and the whole assembly of Israel while they were weeping at the entrance to the tent of meeting. When Phinehas son of Eleazar, the son of Aaron, the priest, saw this, he left the assembly, took a spear in his hand and followed the Israelite into the tent. He drove the spear into both of them, right through the Israelite man and into the woman's stomach. Then the plague against the Israelites was stopped; but those who died in the plague numbered 24,000.

The Lord said to Moses, "Phinehas son of Eleazar, the son of Aaron, the priest, has turned my anger away from the Israelites. Since he was as zealous for my honor among them as I am, I did not put an end to them in my zeal. Therefore tell him I am making my covenant of peace with him. He and his descendants will have a covenant of a lasting priesthood, because he was zealous for the honor of his God and made atonement for the Israelites."

Numbers 25:6-13

Paul calls his and his peoples' zeal in the current situation "without knowledge." What made his violent persecution any different than Moses' and Phinehas'? What made the Israelites of his day any different for rejecting the Christians and their Christ?

As it turns out, it is one thing to be zealous for the name of the Lord and follow what He says and another thing entirely to oppose Him. Unfortunately for Paul and his fellow Israelites, they were actually opposing the one they thought they were serving.

Somewhere along the way, the leaders of the Israelites had come up with a new set of laws, that for the most part, superseded God's Law. They spent millions of collective hours studying God's Word to find ways to justify what they wanted to believe, instead of searching His Word to know Him. Their entire educational system was a lie, and they didn't even know it. The knowledge they stored up for themselves was all wrong.

Paul tells us that the Israelites had established a righteousness of their own, instead of chasing after God's righteousness. It was this bent toward self-justification that caused their hearts to become dull to God's love. It was this dullness that caused them to reject God Himself, when He appeared before them in human form as Jesus.

RIGHTEOUSNESS
10:5-13

Moses spoke in Deuteronomy 30 that God's righteousness and His decrees aren't all that far away from us. Actually, they're right in our mouths and in our hearts (v8). Paul then gives us one of the most famous passages in Romans, and maybe even the Bible:

If you declare with your mouth, "Jesus is Lord," and believe in your heart that God raised him from the dead, you will be saved.

Romans 10:9

Our justification before God comes from the faith we possess in our hearts, and our salvation comes from the confession we make before other people. This justification through Jesus is true knowledge. Anything that denies Him is not knowledge, but foolishness, and it is that knowledge that Jesus saves us, that makes us all one; both Jew and Gentile.

MESSENGERS
10:14-21

To believe in Jesus, we must first be given the opportunity to hear about Him. Paul's life was spent for this very reason, to be a herald of the good news of Jesus's justification and salvation.

As it turns out, the Lord made it clear through His prophets in the Old Testament that His people Israel would reject Him. Paul quotes for us the Psalms, Isaiah and Moses to show us that God saw this coming. It was part of His plan to use the Gentiles—"a nation that has no understanding" (v19).

Even though Israel was going to reject God, it didn't mean that God was going to reject them.

ROMANS CHAPTER 11

I HAVE RESERVED FOR MYSELF...
11:1-10

Even though he deserved God's rejection, God still chose and accepted Paul. Paul knew that there were still many more Jews that had or would turn to faith in Jesus.

Just like in the days of Elijah, there were in Paul's day, and in our day too, Jews whose hearts are tender toward Jesus. Like Elijah, we may not always personally see them, but they are most certainly there. Today, in fact, there are more Jewish Christians than ever before in human history.

The tragedy of Romans 11 is that there were so many Israelites who willingly gave themselves over to a "spirit of stupor," (v8). But even still, the Lord chose for Himself those who would be redeemed. He did this from Paul's day right up until now.

LIFE FROM THE DEAD
11:11-16

Paul tells us that it is because Israel rejected God that salvation has been offered to the Gentiles. At this point, Paul gets very direct in his address to Gentile Christians—an address that many Gentile Christian leaders did not pay attention to through the centuries.

Paul knew that his calling was to the Gentiles, but all the while his secret ambition was also to cause his fellow Jews to turn green with envy when they saw the favor and grace on Gentiles that they knew was from the One True God. He hoped that they would see the evidence of God's grace on Gentile Christians and long for that same favor from their Creator.

One of the most important statements that Paul makes in Romans is this: "For if their rejection brought reconciliation to the world, what will their acceptance be but life from the dead? If the part of the dough offered as firstfruits is holy, then the whole batch is holy; if the root is holy, so are the branches" (v15-16). The day that the Jews accept Jesus will be the greatest day of blessing in human history.

That will be in no small part due to the prophecy that Jesus declared on His ascension to Jerusalem:

> *For I tell you, you will not see me again until you say, 'Blessed is he who comes in the name of the Lord.'"*
>
> *Matthew 23:39*

Jesus told us that He would not return until His people, the Israelites, proclaimed with their mouth that Jesus was, in truth, their Messiah. The day that they accept him, as Paul tells us here in Romans 11, will truly be a day of "life from the dead!"

WILD OLIVE BRANCHES
11:17-24

Paul now gives us a warning that has been scarcely heeded throughout Christian history. He creates the analogy of an olive tree, of which a Jewish "branch" was pruned off because it lacked fruit, and to which a Gentile "wild branch" was grafted back in.

Paul warns us that we Gentiles are not the root. The root is and always will be Jewish. We have been grafted into a Jewish religion, something we should be careful not to forget. The warning to us is that if a Jewish branch can be removed, so can a Gentile branch.

That is a terrifying thought. A logical question when reading this passage is, can we lose our salvation? The answer to that is a longer discussion than we have time for here, but that's not the point Paul is making here. Paul is specifically talking about walking in the fear of the Lord—something incredibly necessary for salvation.

We are warned clearly to tremble with fear. That may sound like something completely contrary to the modern teaching that Jesus loves you, but it is completely complementary to it. Solomon, over a thousand years before Paul, made this bold statement:

> *The fear of the LORD is the beginning of wisdom, and knowledge of the Holy One is understanding.*

> *Proverbs 9:10*

Many times the terrible blow of this fear is softened by calling it "reverence," but that is not what the Bible intends for us to understand. It is truly a terrifying reality to understand that there is one who quite literally holds our eternal fate in His hands. We really could end up in hell—an eternity of suffering, punishment and banishment from God's presence. The fact that hell is a very real option for us should cause us to be afraid.

That fear is necessary for us to approach God in the proper fashion. If we do not truly understand the fate that awaits us, we will more than likely look at the Good News of Jesus' salvation as just regular news. It is much easier to forget that we must continue in faith, as Paul warns us, if we do not remember the truly fearful future that could await us.

Paul calls this the "kindness and sternness" of God. He is kind because there is a way to escape this horrible future, but there is no other way to escape it except by the way He has prescribed. We cannot form our own way to God. We cannot justify ourselves, redefine sin or find some alternate path. It will not work.

The Jews, who were attached to this "cultivated olive tree" chose to abandon their roots and find new ways to justify themselves from sin, and they were cut off. If God did not spare the natural children, why would He spare those He has adopted into His chosen family?

The great news is that fear of God is not what rules our lives as believers, it is only what brings us to God. Solomon said that fear was the "beginning" of wisdom. Fear is how we come to God, but joy is what we learn in His presence.

You make known to me the path of life; you will fill me with joy in your presence, with eternal pleasures at your right hand.

Psalm 16:11

ISRAEL'S FULL SALVATION
11:25-32

The church had a dramatic shift in Paul's day from being 100% Jewish to almost exclusively Gentile. Paul was afraid of the Gentiles becoming conceited by this reality, and for good reason. Paul no doubt saw this growing in his day, and from that time until now the church has been largely very antisemitic. There are entire theological systems that believe the Jews gave away their favored status before God and that the Gentile church has replaced the Jews as God's chosen people.

This was very troubling to Paul for several reasons. He probably saw what would be done to his people if this took root, but he also feared that the Gentiles would miss the true meaning behind the Jews' rejection.

Paul knew that there was coming a day when every single Jewish person would acknowledge Jesus as their Messiah. There are far too many Old Testament prophecies about this to list here, but Paul quotes Isaiah to back this up. There is coming a day when Jesus will return and take away the sin of His chosen people—specifically Israel.

As Gentiles, we should look to that day when all Israel will be saved with great anticipation, because it will be one of the greatest moments in human history—not just for Jews—but for Gentiles as well. It will be the moment when Jesus returns and ushers in perfect peace and governance for all eternity.

THE MIND OF THE LORD (DOXOLOGY)
11:33-36

The thought of God's people fully accepting Jesus causes Paul to go into one of the most beautiful passages in the New Testament. This excitement produces what we now call Paul's doxology, or his overwhelming statement of worship to God.

The way that God has orchestrated His salvation for Jews and Gentiles is beyond human comprehension. Paul had very clear revelation about how God planned to save His people, but very little insight as to why. This doxology is Paul's exclamation of that great mystery that is the ways in which God does things. They are so very different than the ways we would do things, and our small minds are so incredibly incapable of understanding God's plan from beginning to end.

But one thing is for certain, and we can see it throughout the arc of history: God is good, and He deserves all our glory and honor forever!

Don't forget to read Romans this week!
Visit 10WeekBible.com for more resources including daily podcasts, videos and more.

ROMANS 12-13

STUDY QUESTIONS

1. How do faith and works play out in the life of a Christian?

2. How do we show that we love the Lord with all our heart, mind and strength?

3. Why would Paul tell us to hate evil? Do you feel like you *hate* evil? What does that actually look like in our lives today?

4. How should we treat others in light of the salvation that Jesus has offered us? Is this something you struggle with? What are some ways you can grow in this?

5. How can we think of ourselves with sober judgment without being self-condemning?

6. How should submission look in the life of a Christian, and why?

7. What are some ways we can submit to our governing authorities? What are some times we should refuse to submit to them?

COMMENTARY NOTES

ROMANS CHAPTER 12

RENEWING OF YOUR MIND
12:1-2

The first sentence of chapter twelve says more about how Paul views grace and works than almost anything else in Scripture. For centuries, there has been an ongoing tension between grace and works. The difference of liberty and law has defined some of the greatest conflicts in church history.

So how does Paul see the difference? What place do works have in the life of the believer? Are they necessary for salvation? Are they necessary after salvation? In one short sentence, Paul sums it up with dramatic eloquence.

"In view of God's mercy..." (v1)

Paul makes sure that we understand that what follows here is all because of God's great mercy for us, not toward the attainment of it. We do not resist the "pattern of this world" so that we can please God enough to save us, but because it is the only rational response to the incomparable gift of grace that we have been given.

When we think about our destiny before God's grace, and then the salvation from that destiny we have been granted, nothing in this world makes sense except whole-hearted devotion to God with everything we have: our time, our money, our minds and our energy.

Jesus quotes Scripture this way:

"Teacher, which is the greatest commandment in the Law?"

Jesus replied: " 'Love the Lord your God with all your heart and with all your soul and with all your mind.' This is the first and greatest commandment.

Matthew 22:36-38

This is the greatest commandment in the Bible, but it becomes less of a commandment now and more of just common sense. We were rebellious sinners destined for an eternity of punishment and separation from God, but we have been offered an eternity in God's glorious presence, with gifts and authority beyond our wildest imagination. Loving the Lord like this in light of that knowledge doesn't seem like much of a commandment anymore.

Living a life of holiness—a different life from what the world around us looks like—is our act of worship. We often think of worship as the thing we do on Sunday mornings, but Paul makes it clear that our worship doesn't happen at a place or time on a certain day. No, our worship is the decision we make to live differently as a result of this incredible salvation we have been offered.

People often wonder how we can know what God's will is for our lives. How can we know what God wants of us? Paul offers us the easy answer in this most densely-packed section of Romans.

As we reject the way of this world, our mind will, over time, be transformed and we will know what God's will is. It is just that simple (and that hard). As we grow in our ability to reject the sinful ways of this world, we will more easily be able to ascertain God's plan for our lives. His will is learned through days, weeks, months and years of seeking the Lord.

Think about how many people who have either rejected God or say they are Christians, but live far away from God. How many of those people in your life seem like they have confidence in their life's direction?

Now think about the older people in your church that have followed the Lord closely all their lives. Does that person (or people) seem like they have a better grasp on the meaning and purpose for their life?

We do not serve the Lord to earn our salvation, but because nothing else makes sense once we have been saved. One of the extra benefits of working to live our lives differently than we did before we were saved is that we grow in confidence, peace and happiness, because we know we are on the right path.

BE COOL
12:3-8

"Think of yourself with sober judgment" (v3) is sound advice from Paul, no matter who or where you are. Human nature causes us all to feel underpaid, under-appreciated and under-utilized. It is much easier to look at the negatives in situations rather than the positives, so instead of naturally defaulting to humility, we actually puff ourselves up.

When we feel like we're not getting everything we deserve, we are moving in the opposite direction of humility. That's not always a bad thing, especially if we really are being slighted or if we are in a place that needs to change. Sometimes that discomfort is what gets us to start thinking about the new thing the Lord may have for us.

Where that thinking goes wrong is when we do not properly self-evaluate and we get too big a head on our shoulders. We have all seen this happen in multiple spheres in our lives: at work, at home and even at church.

Organizations are not very well-suited for reproducing or honoring things that aren't at their core mission. If your church has made itself into a place that focuses on teaching, hospitality probably isn't something that's going to be high on anyone's list of importance. But a leader that recognizes that they need people who operate in different giftings than themselves is a powerful leader.

The Lord has given us all gifting, and if it is serving, as opposed to prophesying, we should do it to the best of our ability with the proper humility. When we have confidence in our value before God because of His redemption of us, not because of our service to Him, then it makes finding our place in this world much easier. It makes being part of the body of Christ a powerful thing.

LOVE WELL
12:9-13

Paul begins by telling us to love and hate at the same time. He is appealing to some of our most visceral emotions. The idea of hating what is evil is an odd concept. Hate is almost always negative, but here Paul is using it as a double-negative of sorts. Hating evil is enough of a paradox that it should cause us to pause for a moment to consider what he means.

To hate evil is to love righteousness, which is exactly what Paul is equating. What Paul wants us to do here, however, is not to know that connection, but to feel it. If we can actually form a proper sense of justice in our hearts, it will guide us exquisitely.

Many people say they honor justice and mercy, but they seem to lack a sense of self-awareness that would expose their own injustices and lack of grace and mercy to others. If we can truly learn to hate evil and love righteousness, we will much more easily see it in ourselves. That is the backbone of what Paul is saying here.

We can only honor others above ourselves when we see ourselves in light of our true spiritual condition—beggars before a merciful God. When we see ourselves correctly, it becomes much easier to treat other people as they deserve. It becomes much easier to host and care for them as we ourselves have been cared for by our Father.

ROMANS' SERMON ON THE MOUNT
12:14-21

Nowhere in the New Testament is there a more powerful sermon than Jesus' Sermon on the Mount. (Matthew 5-7) Here in Romans, Paul reiterates many of the core ideas of that sermon; things that are all summed up in Jesus' Golden Rule: treat others like you would want to be treated.

That forces us into a position of greater humility because when we think of how we want to be treated, it will temper our tongue and subdue our rage. And that rage—that desire for revenge—even that Paul asks us to lay down. What he asks us to lay down is counter-intuitive to many Christians, though.

Paul tells us not to take revenge, but to make room for God's wrath. A desire for revenge consumes and destroys us, but God, in His perfect justice, will actually take revenge for us when the wicked people who harm us deserve it.

Paul quotes Deuteronomy 32:35 where the Lord first told us He would be our avenger. In the same way that Jesus tells us to "turn the other cheek," Paul here tells us to feed our enemies if we see them hungry.

Heaping burning coals on our enemies' heads may not seem like a kind thing to do, but it evokes the emotions that we truly have about our enemies. In a figurative sense, by showing kindness to those who have worked to harm us, we will actually cause them to feel the emotions we wish we could force on them.

Repaying someone with good for the evil they have

done to us is actually more satisfying than revenge. It causes the tit-for-tat that they would love to engage in to end, leaving them with nowhere to go. It gives them a sense of ending up without the upper hand, an emotion that truly feels like having hot coals dumped on your head.

ROMANS CHAPTER 13

SUBMISSION
13:1-7

Much has been made of the idea of submission in the past fifty to one hundred years in the church in America, with much of it aimed at wives submitting to husbands. While it is true that wives are commanded to submit to their husbands (Ephesians 5:22), it is also true that husbands are told to submit to each other in the church, including their wives (Ephesians 5:21), and to submit to our governing authorities here in Romans.

Submission is not a command we give to those below us to gain prominence, but a command to all Christians universally. We must think of ourselves in lowly terms because of our reality—that we are sinful beggars before a merciful but just God. Anything less dishonors the salvation that we have been given.

What Paul says about our government is almost unbelievable, though. Think about the most loathsome politician you can remember. Think about how much you disliked them and how horrible they were. You probably don't have to think for very long to recall that person and what they did. Now, reconcile that distaste for them with the fact that Paul says they were given their authority by none other than God Himself!

Yes, in a democracy we get to vote, but the millions of votes of the collective of citizens pale in comparison to the vote of the One who actually has the final say in who rules. No one, great or small, has been given a position of authority unless God has given it to them. It doesn't necessarily mean that God approved of that person or thought them a worthy person to lead—only that He appointed them.

For that reason, when we rebel against our governing authorities, we are actually rebelling against God. That, however, is more proverbial than compelling. We are not held to that in every case. The apostles told the Sanhedrin they could not obey their directive to cease preaching the good news about Jesus:

> *Peter and the other apostles replied: "We must obey God rather than human beings!*
>
> *Acts 5:29*

There are also times when rebellion against outright wickedness is necessary, but that is actually seldom the case with our leaders. They may not always be especially competent or righteous, but when they are not trying to go against the Lord or His Word, then we have this directive to obey.

God has actually given into their hands the ability to punish us. God has, and will continue to, use governing officials to punish, rebuke and reform our hearts.

It is important again to reconcile this teaching with what Solomon had to say about wicked rulers:

> *When the righteous thrive, the people rejoice; when the wicked rule, the people groan.*
>
> *Proverbs 29:2*

If you preach the Gospel of Jesus, you may break man's laws, and that will be okay before God, but if you choose to murder, steal or cheat, then you will never be justified before God and He will use those governing authorities to rebuke and chasten you.

And if this passage couldn't get any worse, Paul even tells us that we should willingly submit our taxes to our governments because we are to think of them as "God's servants!"

That may be the toughest pill to swallow!

LOVE
13:8-10

This is where the Beatles got it mostly right: "love is all you need." When we have a proper definition of what love truly is, then it is truly all we need.

Paul and Jesus both tell us that true love is the fulfillment and embodiment of the Law given in the Old Testament. To walk in love is to walk in agreement with God. You cannot do harm to anyone if you love them, so love will prevent you from falling into sin against others.

The Return of Jesus
13:11-14

One of the primary beliefs of Christians is that Jesus rose from the dead and that He will return again to redeem us to God forever. This return of Jesus turns out to be our greatest hope. Because He has forgiven our sins, He will be back for us again one day.

Because of that reality, we need to make sure that we do not grow complacent in our behavior. Jesus really will return for us, so it is important to live like that is true. We do not need to behave out of fear, although that can be a powerful, and even a positive motivator; but we need to walk in holiness in honor and reverence to the salvation and calling we have.

Again, we do not behave because it earns us favor with God, but because we have been granted favor with God, we should choose to behave as our act of gratitude for it.

Don't forget to read Romans this week!
Visit 10WeekBible.com for more resources including daily podcasts, videos and more.

9

Romans 14-15

Study Questions

1. Do you like it when others nit-pick your life decisions? Do you do the same thing to others?

2. What do you consider "disputable" or "debatable" matters? What do you consider foundational things that cannot be compromised?

3. What would it look like to lay down your own preferences for others?

4. What are some things that you believe would be sin for you but maybe not others?

5. How can you love those around you who don't hold the same convictions as you in "debatable" matters?

6. How can you continue to enjoy the things you don't believe are sin without "destroying" those around you?

7. Why do you think it was so important for Paul not to spend time evangelizing in places where the gospel had already been proclaimed? How do you feel that may relate to your life today?

COMMENTARY NOTES

ROMANS CHAPTER 14

LIVE AND LET LIVE
14:1-12

To one extent or another, almost all people would love to be able to control, or at least give their opinion about, how other people live. There is something within us that causes us to want other people to care what we think about their choices. For many people (although not all), this requires intentionality to keep their noses out of other peoples' business.

Unfortunately, not everyone is intentional. We have all had those people offer unsolicited advice that is worth the price we paid for it. Maybe we've been that person. We may think we're being helpful, but in most matters, people are picking the wrong things to give their input about.

What we are talking about is not the kind of situation where people need intervention. Those are good times to meddle and get in the middle of someone's business. What we are talking about are relatively unimportant matters like what kind of food they eat; what kind of disciplinary tactics they take with their children (shy of actual abuse).

Paul makes it clear here that we are all at different places in our journey of faith in God. Note that what Paul does not mean is different belief systems or religions, but in the amount of faith we have in the One True God. Since we are at different places in that journey, we may not always understand where someone else is coming from. We may not have their history and background, so it can be difficult (read: impossible) to judge their hearts or motives.

How many times have people who refuse to drink alcohol been judged as prudish or hyper-religious when they may be, in fact, a recovering alcoholic? How often are people in church who do drink considered licentious?

Paul uses the phrase "disputable matters" (v1) as rendered in the NIV ("doubtful things" in NKJV). This is the key phrase to understanding this entire chapter. Paul is not saying we shouldn't confront people who believe or teach others that they don't need to accept Jesus to be right with God. He is saying that we shouldn't treat that the same as someone who believes they shouldn't eat meat.

Rupertus Meldenius coined a phrase in the 17th century that many believers adopted in light of Paul's words:

In the Essentials; Unity.

In the Non-Essentials; Liberty.

In all things; Love.

That is the essence of what Paul is admonishing us toward in this passage. We should not, and cannot, simply watch as friends and loved ones allow their lives to be ravaged by sin and darkness without saying something. We cannot let them be led away by heresy.

106

Those are the essentials.

By the same token, we cannot place the same importance on things that don't carry the same weight—the
non-essentials. How someone raises their children,
how they eat or what kind of worship music their
church uses are not in the same category. Not even
close.

For those matters, we should mostly keep quiet. We
should treat each other as Paul directs us here: that we
will each answer to God for the little decisions we
make. We serve our Master, and He has not given all
of us the same charge or responsibilities. We all have
the same calling to accept His Son, Jesus, but we do
not all have the same assignment in life.

LET LIVE AND LOVE
14:13-23

Paul doesn't stop with charging us with keeping our
noses out of other peoples' business. He actually goes
a step further by telling us to know what is going on
with those around us, and making sure we are not in-
tentionally doing anything to make them stumble.

With someone we know well enough to know that
they think drinking is sinful, is it worth it to offer
them a drink? Or pork to an abstainer? Or meat to a
vegetarian? Paul says that these things are not wrong
or unclean in themselves, but that if someone else
views them as unclean, something entirely different
comes to play.

Paul goes so far to say that when we do these things,

we are not acting in love for that person, but out of selfishness, and everything done outside of love is sin.

One way this plays out is between Gentile Christians and Messianic Jews (Jewish Christians). While the Bible is very clear for Gentiles—that they are not required to abide by the Law of Moses in regards to what they eat and drink—it is much less clear for Messianic Jews. Paul believes that he (a Jew) is okay to eat and drink anything, but not all Messianic Jews feel that way, and outside of this passage, the Bible is less clear about that.

Many Gentile Christians have caused Messianic Jews great heartache by telling them it is okay for them to eat pork, or any other non-kosher food. Instead of honoring a Messianic Jew's desire to live as the Lord has specifically called them, Gentiles sometimes "destroy" them, as Paul says.

No food or drink is worth that.

Another way this could play out is if a Western Christian tried to convince an Indian Christian that it is okay to eat meat. Even though the Indian Christian has moved beyond a Hindu teaching on reincarnation, the act of not eating meat for a lifetime may be so ingrained in them it still feels wrong. Meat is not worth convincing someone else to act against their conscience.

Paul actually tells us that it is not the act of them eating or not eating that is sin, but sin happens when we convince them to act against their conscience.

What all of this does not mean is that we need to never eat or drink or do something that others find offensive or believe to be sinful. If that were the case, we couldn't eat or drink anything. What Paul means is that when we relate to one another, we must make every effort to leave behind those offensive things.

If you know that there is a Messianic Jew in your church, don't bring ham to the church pot-luck. For you, ham is fine, so just eat it at home. If you're inviting someone you know who thinks eating meat is wrong, don't take them out to lunch for barbecue. Go have barbecue by yourself or with your own family.

There is something within our human nature that makes us feel that if something is okay for us, it should be okay for everyone. Paul is asking us to love others in such a way that we are willing to lay down our own personal preferences to protect the conscience and walk with God others have.

And again, what this does not apply to is if someone thinks it is okay to serve both Jesus and Buddha. Or to worship New-Age spirits and God at the same time. Paul is not asking us to live and let live in that situation. In those cases, it is not love to allow someone to continue in destructive deception.

One of the greatest ways to walk out this tension between love and liberty is to bathe everything in prayer. If we are praying for others and asking the Holy Spirit to lead us how to best relate to them and treat them, we will more likely get it wrong much more often than we get it wrong.

ROMANS CHAPTER 15

THE MIND OF CHRIST
15:1-13

The "law of love", as Paul calls it, should cause us to accept each other in the same way that Christ has accepted us. Again, this does not mean allowing people in our midst to believe in wrong things about Jesus unchallenged. What it means is that, outside of the fundamental teachings about Jesus and salvation, we must show love and grace to one another.

Jesus loved us even while we were yet sinners. And even after we have given our lives to Jesus, He continues to love us even though we continue to sin and hold on to many ideas and theologies that He doesn't. We must learn that same love and tolerance for other believers.

Jesus was our model for this. In His humility, He chose to absorb and bear the reproach and insults of those who hated God—even the people who claimed to serve Him! How much more should we show love to those who truly love Jesus, then?

Paul begins this chapter by speaking to those who are "strong." Rather cunningly, Paul knows he is speaking to everyone. Deep down, who considers themselves weak? Not many. Most people naturally consider themselves strong. Most people, as Paul has already told us, think of themselves more highly than they should. So when Paul says that "we who are strong ought to bear with the failings of the weak and not to please ourselves," (v1), he is speaking to all of us.

All of us should look to those around us and think and pray how we can serve and love them best. How can we strengthen our friends and neighbors, especially those within the church?

As Paul quotes several Old Testament passages, we see where the intent of Romans 14-15 lies. He has been speaking to the differences between Jews and Gentiles. He is asking the Jewish Christians to lay down their own preferences so that the Gentiles may not be "destroyed."

Centuries later, Gentile Christians should turn this script around and view themselves as those who should lay themselves down for the benefit of others, other Gentiles included. How glorious would it be if we could, by how we live our lives, gather in many to know God?

We may think that laying ourselves down to build others up may feel self-defeating, but Paul tells us just the opposite. When we lay our lives down for others, we actually end up filled with greater joy, peace and power. We will end this passage with his own words, possibly some of the most beautiful in all of Romans:

May the God of hope fill you with all joy and peace as you trust in him, so that you may overflow with hope by the power of the Holy Spirit.

Romans 15:13

WHY I HAVEN'T VISITED
15:14-22

Paul is writing the book of Romans to a group of Christians he hasn't yet visited. At this time, they are mainly Jewish Christians, but Paul knows that will soon change.

The reason Paul hasn't yet visited the Christians in Rome is because there is already a growing church there. Paul made a conscious decision to only travel and minister in places where the Gospel hadn't yet been preached.

When Paul tells the Romans that he had proclaimed the gospel from "Jerusalem all the way around to Illyricum," (v19) what he is saying is that he has seen the Gentiles reached around most of the Eastern Mediterranean. Illyricum is what we call modern-day Bosnia and Herzegovina.

ROME AND SPAIN
15:23-33

It is for this reason that Paul hasn't visited Rome, because he is only interested in reaching Gentile populations with no active church. It is for the same reason that even when he does travel to Rome, he hopes that it is only a stopover on his way to Spain—somewhere further into the Gentile world that the Gospel hadn't made it to yet.

We know through Luke's account in the book of Acts that Paul does end up in Rome, but unfortunately as a prisoner. The book of Acts ends with Paul spending two years in Rome and no conclusion of whether or not Paul lived or died or did ever get to visit Spain.

Paul also lets us us know when he wrote the book of Romans. It was on his way to Jerusalem, before his arrest, as we read about in Acts 20-21. In Acts, it becomes clear that Paul knows he will be arrested in Jerusalem, but it is unclear whether Paul knew that when he wrote this letter to the Romans.

Because of Paul's request for prayer, he knew that it was at least going to be dangerous for him to visit Jerusalem. He knew that there were wicked people there who wanted him dead, but maybe he didn't yet know how serious the situation was.

From the text of the Bible, we do not know what happened to Paul after Acts ends. A few scholars think that he was executed by Caesar when he initially stood trial, but not many. The most prevalent story about Paul is that he was exonerated by Nero in Rome after spending two years in house arrest and that he did eventually make his way to Spain.

Some think that after his travels in Spain, he was on his way back to Jerusalem or Antioch and stopped back in Rome. By that time, things had changed, and Paul was arrested along with all the other Christians in Rome and was executed by Nero along with Peter in the mass-crucifixions that Nero held when he blamed the Christians for the great fire of Rome.

Don't forget to read Romans this week!
Visit 10WeekBible.com for more resources including daily
podcasts, videos and more.

ROMANS 16

STUDY QUESTIONS

1. Why do you think the greetings and names of people in the Bible are recorded for all eternity?

2. What are the ways we can show others in our churches and those who have moved on the same kind of love and affection as Paul does here?

3. What are the true dangers of division in church? How can we avoid it?

4. After reading all of Romans, how would you define faith now?

5. How would you define obedience?

6. What is the relationship of obedience and faith as Paul outlines in Romans? How does that affect our love for God and one another?

7. What do you feel will be your response to reading Romans? How has this study changed you?

COMMENTARY NOTES

ROMANS CHAPTER 16

GREETINGS

Paul ends the book of Romans in much the same way his other epistles end: with greetings. The greetings here and in other epistles are truly amazing things. We can read Romans and other books in the Bible and forget that they were written to real people with real emotions.

The love that Paul shows to these very real people is truly touching and endlessly fascinating. For all eternity, these people's names and deeds are recorded in God's Word, and that is no small thing. Instead of rushing through the last chapters of Paul's epistles, we could learn from the tender affection and brotherly love the early church had for one another.

PHOEBE
16:1-2

Paul begins with Phoebe, a woman from Cenchreae. He is obviously grateful for Phoebe because she has financially supported him and other people. She is on her way to Rome (possibly to deliver this letter?), and Paul is asking that the church there accept her. Sending letters of commendation or recommendation were common in this day, but there is something special about having that commendation be recorded for all eternity.

PRISCILLA AND AQUILA
16:3-4

We read about Priscilla and her husband Aquila first in Acts 18. Paul becomes close friends with the two because they all make tents on the side to earn extra money to support their evangelism.

They were from Rome, but when Paul met them, they had been exiled from Rome by Emperor Claudius. They have obviously returned back now and Paul sends his old friends warm greetings.

OTHER GREETINGS
16:5-16

Epenetus was the first convert from Asia; what we now call southwestern Turkey. He has now moved to Rome, and Paul sends his personal greetings.

It is not clear whether Paul is calling Andronicus and Junia apostles here, or whether he means that they are commended by all the apostles. Each translation struggles with this. Either way, Paul shows his love for them.

We know little about Mary, Ampliatus, Urbanus, Stachys, Apelles, Herodion, Tryphena, Tryphosa, Persis, Rufus, Asyncritus, Phlegon, Hermes, Patrobas, Hermas, Philogus, Julia, Nereus and his sister, Olympas or the households of Aristobulus and Narcissus.

What we do know is that their names are recorded forever in memories here and we will meet them one day in the presence of God.

May we learn to love to the same extent in our churches today that we would commend old friends and co-laborers to one another that have moved on from our presence.

Final Warnings
16:17-20

Paul, like a good father with little time left, emphasizes the danger of division between them. It can feel like the only thing consistent in church life throughout the ages is the struggle we all have to truly love one another, but in reality the church has been far better at loving than at fighting one another. The problem is that we tend to focus on the fight instead of the love.

Paul starts and ends this chapter with love, and spares only a few words of warning in between. Those who oppose the teaching of the Bible (what Paul has taught the Romans) are not just troublemakers, but self-serving and rebellious against Jesus. Paul says they are not actually Christians, because they have rejected Jesus in lieu of their own desires.

Paul makes it clear that he and everyone else knows that the Romans are obedient to the Lord, but he still warns them to stay away from these types of people.

He finishes with one final reminder: that in the end, Satan loses and God wins.

GREETINGS FROM THOSE WITH PAUL
16:21-24

Timothy is apparently with Paul when he is writing this letter, as are other Jewish men named Lucious, Jason and Sosipater. What we also find out is that Paul has dictated this entire letter to his traveling companion, Tertius, who actually wrote the letter of Romans.

The final greetings come from Gaius, Erastus and Quartus, most probably all men of means and standing. The fact that Erastus is mentioned as the public works director should cause us to pause. These people were not so different than we are today.

Our cities (of reasonable size) all have public works directors today. In Paul's day, the Romans actually had a fairly sophisticated system of government and bureaucracy that ran relatively smoothly. They employed engineering and construction to greatly enhance the lives of their citizens. Many Roman aqueducts still stand to this day: a testimony of the ancient public works directors.

CONCLUSION
16:25-27

Paul concludes the book with a beautiful statement of glory to God. In Romans, he has covered many topics, but this sums up his desire behind this book incredibly well.

Paul wants the Gentiles to come to the obedience God that only comes from faith. This one concluding statement makes Romans that much easier to understand in its whole: that obedience to God is our requirement, but that we only attain it through faith.

We have seen throughout this book that every objection people have to obedience using Romans to justify it has been shot down by Paul himself, and here again once more. We cannot be made right with God without obedience to Him, but neither can we attain obedience to Him through our adherence to the Old Testament Law.

Faith—the "confidence in what we hope for and assurance about what we do not see"—this is how we learn obedience to God. This is the only thing that makes us right before God. As Paul said in chapter 15, anything apart from faith is sin.

We cannot earn God's favor and forgiveness, but we also cannot turn a blind eye to it once we have accepted it. True acceptance of God's forgiveness changes us and causes us to long for obedience to Him. We may fail and stumble, but it becomes our objective—again, not to earn God's favor, but as the only rational response to how great a salvation we have been given.

This is the message of Romans. This is the very thing that has changed millions of lives throughout the past 2,000 years. This is the hope that we have:

That we are saved by faith through grace. (Paraphrased from Ephesians 2:8)

If you feel that you have never experienced that salvation that comes by faith through grace, please reach out to the people of the local church you are doing this study with. If you are reading this alone in personal study and you have never accepted this salvation, please reach out to me by email at me@Darren-Hibbs.com. I would love to help walk you through the exciting steps to knowing this love and peace that comes from faith in Jesus.

Don't forget to read Romans this week!
Visit 10WeekBible.com for more resources including daily podcasts, videos and more.

Reading Chart

WEEK 1
- ☐ Day 1: Romans 1-2
- ☐ Day 2: Romans 3-5
- ☐ Day 3: Romans 6-7
- ☐ Day 4: Romans 8-10
- ☐ Day 5: Romans 11-13
- ☐ Day 6: Romans 14-16

WEEK 2
- ☐ Day 1: Romans 1-2
- ☐ Day 2: Romans 3-5
- ☐ Day 3: Romans 6-7
- ☐ Day 4: Romans 8-10
- ☐ Day 5: Romans 11-13
- ☐ Day 6: Romans 14-16

WEEK 3
- ☐ Day 1: Romans 1-2
- ☐ Day 2: Romans 3-5
- ☐ Day 3: Romans 6-7
- ☐ Day 4: Romans 8-10
- ☐ Day 5: Romans 11-13
- ☐ Day 6: Romans 14-16

WEEK 4
- ☐ Day 1: Romans 1-2
- ☐ Day 2: Romans 3-5
- ☐ Day 3: Romans 6-7
- ☐ Day 4: Romans 8-10
- ☐ Day 5: Romans 11-13
- ☐ Day 6: Romans 14-16

WEEK 5
- ☐ Day 1: Romans 1-2
- ☐ Day 2: Romans 3-5
- ☐ Day 3: Romans 6-7
- ☐ Day 4: Romans 8-10
- ☐ Day 5: Romans 11-13
- ☐ Day 6: Romans 14-16

WEEK 6
- ☐ Day 1: Romans 1-2
- ☐ Day 2: Romans 3-5
- ☐ Day 3: Romans 6-7
- ☐ Day 4: Romans 8-10
- ☐ Day 5: Romans 11-13
- ☐ Day 6: Romans 14-16

WEEK 7
- ☐ Day 1: Romans 1-2
- ☐ Day 2: Romans 3-5
- ☐ Day 3: Romans 6-7
- ☐ Day 4: Romans 8-10
- ☐ Day 5: Romans 11-13
- ☐ Day 6: Romans 14-16

WEEK 8
- ☐ Day 1: Romans 1-2
- ☐ Day 2: Romans 3-5
- ☐ Day 3: Romans 6-7
- ☐ Day 4: Romans 8-10
- ☐ Day 5: Romans 11-13
- ☐ Day 6: Romans 14-16

WEEK 9
- ☐ Day 1: Romans 1-2
- ☐ Day 2: Romans 3-5
- ☐ Day 3: Romans 6-7
- ☐ Day 4: Romans 8-10
- ☐ Day 5: Romans 11-13
- ☐ Day 6: Romans 14-16

WEEK 10
- ☐ Day 1: Romans 1-2
- ☐ Day 2: Romans 3-5
- ☐ Day 3: Romans 6-7
- ☐ Day 4: Romans 8-10
- ☐ Day 5: Romans 11-13
- ☐ Day 6: Romans 14-16

ABOUT THE AUTHOR

Darren Hibbs is the founder of the 10 Week Bible Study. He believes that the methodology of studying the Bible in this book can radically transform your life with God.

By filling your heart and mind with the Word of God first and foremost, you will better know God's heart than if your Bible knowledge comes primarily from sermons or even the commentary provided within this book. There is nothing more powerful for transformation than a people who know for themselves the Word of God.

Darren's heart burns to bring a message of hope to a lost and broken world through the immeasurable love of Jesus. It is his heart that the church will grow in love for God and embrace His love and power so that the lost will see and hear the good news about Jesus as they see it change us.

Darren writes regularly and can be reached at
www.DarrenHibbs.com.

Other Titles by 10 Week Bible

Titles in Print & Digital Formats:
1 Samuel
2 Samuel
Esther
Daniel
John
Acts
Romans
Revelation

For a full and up-to-date list of titles in print, as well as for bookstore ordering information, visit 10WeekBible.com

Find out more at 10WeekBible.com

10 WEEK BIBLE STUDY PODCAST

If you have enjoyed this study, you may also enjoy the 10 Week Bible Study Podcast. This is a five day a week broadcast designed to help you get through each book of the Bible ten weeks at a time. It includes the reading of the entire book being studied once and helpful commentary to encourage your personal reading and study of God's Word.

You can listen to the podcast on any platform on the go or at home. For a list of easy links to subscribe to the podcast, visit 10WeekBible.com.

There, you can also subscribe to the broadcast on You-Tube.

Watch on

Join our group at